"You can't read this welcome acc[...] East Africa, Ludwig Krapf, and b[...] sued the vision of the conversion [...] great, no obstacle could make hir[...] of his first wife so soon after arriving in Mombasa will move you to tears. What realism! What faith! What grace of God! In many ways taking the gospel to the world is so much easier today. So where are the Krapfs of today? So much of the world is still unreached. May such an account stir the hearts of many of God's people."

Keith Underhill
Founding pastor at Trinity Baptist Church, Nairobi,
now retired and living in England

"Like all good missionary biographies, *Johann Ludwig Krapf: His Life and Legacy* is well researched, magnifies the Saviour and demonstrates the lasting impact of a life of sacrifice, lived attempting great things for God and expecting great things from God."

David Morrow
Area Director, UFM Worldwide (Ireland)

"Through many years and many trials on the mission field, my wife and I have always reminded each other, 'The gospel costs— but it's worth it!" This story of Ludwig Krapf beautifully illustrates that truth. I am inspired by the high cost he was willing to pay for the gospel, convinced of its beauty, value, and rescuing power. Krapf pursued the proclamation of the gospel in East Africa at great personal expense. I trust your heart will be stirred by his faith, courage, and passion for the gospel."

Rob Trenckmann
Head of Operations, Newton House, Oxford;
Former Country Lead for Josiah Venture, Hungary

"God's Providence is often so unmistakable in hindsight. The story of Johann Ludwig Krapf, detailed by Aaron Dunlop, is blessed with moment-by-moment displays of God's gracious hand over his servant. The Christian life is often one of struggle and hardship, yet the work is the Lord's and his will is accomplished—the frailest vessels behold the choicest wine. As Krapf notes, "how mysterious and marvelous are the Lord's ways"; so it is throughout so many missionary biographies as they reveal the honest conundrum of divine blessing and human failure. We are not for want of former saints but have need to read and explore the ways that God has worked through them—through those who would die on their knees in prayer and conviction. Dunlop's retrieval of Krapf is more than just a detailed biography but a blooming promise of how the Great Shepherd would call his sheep from every nation, including the Oromo tribes. Every church would be wise to include this well-written, delightful, and invigorating biography in her library, surely there is room between the Judsons and the Livinstones."

Christopher Ellis Osterbrock
Pastor, First Baptist Church of Wellsboro, PA;
Author, *What Is Saving Faith?*

Johann Ludwig Krapf

AARON DUNLOP

JOHANN LUDWIG
KRAPF
His Life and Legacy

joshua
press

Published by: Joshua Press, Peterborough, Ontario
www.JoshuaPress.com

Cover design by Chance Faulkner

Paperback ISBN: 978-1-77484-057-3
Ebook ISBN: 978-1-77484-058-0

To Grace, my Shulamite
To James, Bethan, William, Emily and Thomas
… and to the memory of our travels and happy times
together in East Africa

Contents

Foreword

Aaron Dunlop, the author of this latest biography of Dr. Johann Ludwig Krapf, is a missionary in Kitui County of Kenya, East Africa. Like his father, Alan Dunlop, the younger Aaron has distinguished himself as a dedicated and selfless missionary through his work not only in spreading the word of God but also in helping the less fortunate members of the society. His interest in heritage matters has undoubtedly led him to the work on this biography. We at the National Museums of Kenya applaud him for his efforts.

The legacy of Krapf, the first Protestant missionary to East Africa, has long been a matter of discussion. The penetration and spread of Christianity into the interior of East Africa by early missionaries was not an easy task. It required extraordinary determination and commitment for one to attain such documented success. Krapf persevered the difficult challenges of the harsh tropical climate heavily infested with Malaria, language barrier, and the periodic attacks from warring communities.

His first posting by the Church Missionary Society (CMS) was to Ethiopia, but the mission was forced to leave before it was properly established. In Mombasa and its hinterland, together with his companions, he made only a tiny handful of converts. The mission he established became a backwater, and his grand missionary strategy proved a nonstarter. This apparent lack success led the CMS to pause for thought and to conclude that it was natural for draw backs and some discouragement. Due to Krapf's determination and commitment to the service of God, he, together with other missionaries who joined him later in the evangelical mission, continued to pursue the course and managed to

spread the Christian religion into East, Central Africa and beyond.

In transporting Christianity to Africa, Krapf felt he was con-
veying a superior belief system. He took back and shared images
of Africa which stirred a lot of interest that resulted in the scram-
ble for the African continent by colonial powers. He also brought
in secular education, attire, and health-care systems. Furthermore, the linguistic similarity among Bantu languages showed the
potential for future comparative work and could be used to facil-
itate the project of Bible translation. Such a high degree of resem-
blance rendered the prospect of translating the Bible into all the
languages more feasible. The grammar books that he came across,
Arch bell's Tswana grammar and Boyce's Xhosa grammar, influenced Krapf's depiction and also encouraged him to carry on with
his description of the Swahili language.

Dr. Krapf's contribution and its effects, whether scientific or
missionary, can only be grasped in the light of historical, political
events and intellectual climate of his time in which pietism often
played the role of an ideological catalyst. Krapf arrived at a favor-
able moment in East Africa: the region's growing links with western trade networks, the striving for the abolition of slavery, the
project of civilization and mission. His advent to East Africa was
synergetic and finally, despite ambiguities, marked the eve of colonial era. Through his explorations, discoveries and his missionary project, whether deliberately or not, Krapf helped to set the
stage for colonization in East African and stirred European interest in the hitherto neglected "dark continent."

It is through Krapf's perseverance of the difficult challenges
that helped in spreading Christianity into East, Central Africa and
beyond.

In the wake of all these travels in his missionary activities,
Krapf left memorable sites, some of which have been taken over
by the management of the National Museums of Kenya as

heritage sites of National significance. One such site is the Rabai Religious Cultural Site in Kilifi County. This site is arguably one of the earliest Christian sites along the Coast of Kenya and can be referred to as the "Cradle of Christianity in East Africa."

Dr. David Musila,
(National Museums of Kenya, Nairobi)
May 2020

Timeline

1810, January 11	Ludwig Krapf was born in Derendingen, near Tübingen, Germany.
1825/6	Krapf was converted to Christ.
1827	Krapf entered the Basel Missionary Institute.
1834	Krapf graduated from the University of Tübingen, Württemberg.
1837, February 6	Krapf set out on his journey to Ethiopia.
1842, September 22	Krapf married Fraülein Rosine Dietrich in Alexandria, Egypt.
1843, May 26	Rosine prematurely gave birth to a little girl, 'Eneba' *a tear*. The baby died that same day.
1844, January 3	The Krapfs arrived at Mombasa.
1844, June 8	Krapf began a tentative translation of the book of Genesis into Kiswahili.
1844, July 13	Rosine Krapf died of puerperal fever.
1844, July 16	Their second infant daughter was buried alongside Rosine.
1846, June 10	Mr. Rebmann arrives at Mombasa.

Timeline

1849, December 3	Krapf saw Mt. Kenya for the first time.
1850, April 10	Krapf left for Europe (his first furlough).
1850, November 24	Mringe, the first convert was baptised by Erhardt (Krapf was in England).
1851, January 2	The Valedictory Dismissal of Krapf as he returned to Mombasa.
1851, July 11	Krapf set out on his second trip to Ukambani. He made it to the Tana River.
1853	Krapf visited Ethiopia in connection with Bishop Gobet's mission.
1855, September	Krapf retired from the CMS, started a new phase of his missionary Career.
1856	Krapf married his second wife, Charlotte Pelargus.
1860, November 14	Krapf met the committee of the United Methodist Free Churches.
1867–68	Krapf joined the British Expedition to Ethiopia as a translator for Sir Robert Napier.
1869	Krapf married his third wife, Nanette Schmidt von Cannstadt.
1881, November 27	Krapf is found dead on his knees at his bedside on the morning of Advent Sunday.

Introduction

Scattered along the coast of Kenya are a number of iconic historic sites, now part of the rich cultural portfolio of the National Museums of Kenya, and sources of revenue for the Kenyan tourism industry. The most famous of these is Fort Jesus, the 16th century Portuguese fortress. There is also the Vasco da Gama Pillar in Malindi, in memory of the Portuguese explorer, and then there is the Gedi Ruins at Watamu, an ancient Muslim settlement going back to the 13th century.

Many of these historic sites remind us of the attempts to Christianise the coast during the expansion of the Portuguese Empire and ensuing struggle with Islam which expelled Christianity in 1631. In the providence of God, however, it was Protestant Christianity that finally penetrated Africa from the East Coast, and while the historical evidence of this is less conspicuous than the Gedi Ruins or Fort Jesus, the story is nonetheless remarkable, filled with courage, tenacious fortitude and rich in missionary vision, zeal and Christian faith.

On a quiet, narrow street, just across the Harbour from Fort Jesus, is the first Christian missionary grave in East Africa, the resting place of Mrs. Rosine Krapf. She died just a few months after their arrival. Her infant daughter was buried alongside her three days later; she was not given a name. Hidden in the trees, across the street from the graves, is a monument to the memory of Dr. Ludwig Krapf, erected some years after he left Kenya.

Eugene Stock, editor and historian from the Church Missionary Society that sent Krapf to East Africa, said that "Krapf's labours and sufferings in Abyssinia [Ethiopia] and the adjoining kingdom of Shoa [Shewa] form one of the most thrilling chapters of missionary history."[1] Yet, there has been no English biography written on Krapf for seventy years, and no academic research on his missionary labours exists. One wonders why!

Johann Ludwig Krapf was the first missionary to East Africa in modern times and a pioneer in the study of African ethnology, geography and linguistics. Today, he is celebrated in East Africa for opening up the continent for the gospel from the east coast. Monuments, memorials, and museums stand in his honor. Further inland from Mombasa, at Rabai Mpya, is St. Paul's Church, built in 1887, an architectural testimony to the European missionary effort. Today, the original church building houses a small museum, and on the same property the "Rabai Missionary Cemetery," a reminder of the hardship that had to be overcome for the gospel.

Krapf is considered the founding father of the Anglican Church in Kenya. In Europe, he is remembered as the founder of Swahili studies and, still today, his name frequently appears in scholarly African ethnology and linguistic research. In geographical studies, he is credited, along with his colleague, Johannes Rebmann, as the first Europeans to see the snow-capped Mt's. Kilimanjaro and Kenya. In Germany, particularly, Krapf is still revered, and his legacy still forms strong links between the German and Kenyan governments. The German Embassy on Riverside Drive in Nairobi is called "Krapf House."

One biographer, C.G. Richards, wrote, "Amongst the many good men and women, who in the last hundred years have given their services and often their lives in order to carry the spirit of brotherhood to the peoples of East Africa, Ludwig Krapf, the fore-runner of them all, surely stands pre-eminent, and worthy

---

[1] Eugene Stock, *The History of the Church Missionary Society: Its Environment, Its Men and Its Work* (London: Church Missionary Society, 1899), 1:353.

to be remembered."[2] Another writer, the editor of the second edition of Krapf's *Travels* in 1968, stated that the story of Krapf's travels in East Africa was "one of the three or four most significant missionary accounts of nineteenth century Africa."[3]

This biography details how he overcame his early flirtation with Christian mysticism, which almost prevented his missionary intentions. It probes his heart for the unreached Oromo people and reveals his strategic missionary maneuvering and his indomitable courage, fortitude and his faith in a sovereign God in the face of repeated setbacks and personal losses. He never reached the heart of Africa himself, and in this biography, we will consider some of the possible reasons for his lack of success in this. In the end, however, while he conceded the heart of Africa to others, he never gave up on his initial goal. After he had opened up the continent from the east coast for others to follow, he was invalided home to Germany, and, in the providence of God, he was granted the unique opportunity to produce a translation of the Bible in the language of the people he first set out to reach.

Much of the material in this book is taken from Krapf's autobiography. Often, I will quote directly, but there are a few occasions where I will use Krapf's words and phraseology without quoting. Other helpful resources are the numerous works of Eugene Stock on the Church Missionary Society (henceforth referred to as CMS), particularly, "The Missionary Career of Dr. Krapf," published in 1882, just after the death of the great missionary. Stock's writings are especially helpful because he was writing for the CMS and was well acquainted with the work and personnel of the Society. More recent studies which were helpful

---

[2] C.G. Richards, *Krapf: Missionary and Explorer* (London: Thomas Nelson and Sons, 1950), 85

[3] Robert I. Rotberg, "General Editor's Preface," *Travels, Researches and Missionary Labors, During an Eighteen Year's residence in Eastern Africa*, Rprt. 1860 (London: Routledge, 1968), 5.

include the work of Kenyan scholar, Professor Omulokoli, and the work of Roy C. Bridges, history scholar at the University of Aberdeen, printed in the "Introduction" to the second edition of Krapf's "Travels," published in 1968 by Frank Cass and Company.

Other materials used are listed in the bibliography and all were available to me, except the older German works, which include Claus' biography of 1882 and the various writings of Werner Raupp. However, I was happy to find an English biography based on Claus' work by Rev. F. Wilkinson. It was helpful to draw from a number of these biographers, as each one had access to different primary sources, either in England, Germany, or in Kenya. Some of the biographers had access to letters and other material and this has been helpful, and I've used this material where I've been able to find a consensus among the few biographers.

So, it is time for a new English biography for a number of reasons. First, the last English biography, Richard's 1950 work was very brief and is no longer in print. Also, it focused on the expeditions to Ukambani, Usambara and Chagga, rather than the life of Krapf. Second, past biographers, apart from Eugene Stock, focus on certain aspects of his life and do not follow his life chronologically. They therefore miss the development of his character and his missionary strategy for the continent of Africa and the reasons for his return to Europe in 1853. They also avoid dealing with the intense struggles and the rich spiritual life of Krapf. Third, both Kretzmann's and Richards' biographies contain significant errors in dates and activities. Indeed, much of Kretzmann's material is lifted directly out of Wilkinson's 1892 essay in *The Missionary Review of the World*. Fourth, when the last English biography was published in 1950, Kenya had not yet obtained independence. Place names and tribal names have varied spellings across the available literature and many names that were used in colonial times are today regarded offensive and need to be updated. In those places where Krapf uses an obsolete, offensive or archaic word, I have inserted the modern replacement.

It is time for the Christian world, and Kenya in particular, to be reintroduced to this great missionary pioneer—his story is a lost missiological treasure. This, however, is not intended to be an exhaustive treatment. His life and missionary labours deserve more academic research, and this would necessitate access to the various archives, in Cambridge, London, Oxford and Basel. To accomplish a complete biography of Krapf, one would also need to be well acquainted with the life and writings of Johannes Rebmann (1820–1876) and Johann Jakob Erhardt (1823–1901) with whom he worked so closely in Rabai. One would also need a working knowledge of the German language in order to study Krapf's voluminous works and the subsequent scholarly research on Linguistics, ethnography and geography. I will concede that to someone else. The present work will serve to introduce this great missionary to a new generation in the English-speaking world.

A word of thanks is due to Mr. Stephen Kameti for his assistance with Kiswahili and Kikamba place names and various terms. Also, thanks to Dr. David Musila, member of the Kenyan Senate and Chairman of the National Museums of Kenya, who welcomed me and Mr. Kameti to his office at the Nairobi National Museum in July of 2019. We talked about the Krapf legacy and the graves at Mombasa. A special thanks to Dr. Musila for writing a foreword for this important piece of Kenyan history.

Thanks also to Dr. Michael Haykin for recommending this work to the publisher. To Chance Faulkner also, at Joshua Press and to Kayla Wester and Rachel Huffman the copy-editors, for getting it to publication. To Dr. Jochen Eber also, a German biographer of Dr. Krapf (Basel: ArteMedia, 2006) who helped me source photos.

Finally, this biography would not have been possible but for the help and support of my wife, Grace, who read the initial manuscript and gave much-needed advice. Soli Deo Gloria.

Aaron Dunlop
Lisburn, Northern Ireland
Feb. 2021

Chapter 1
Childhood and Early Life

Johann Ludwig Krapf was born on January 11, 1810, in Derendingen, near Tübingen, a largely Protestant region of southern Germany. He was the youngest child of Johann Jakob Krapf, a farmer, and his wife Katherina Maria (nee Braun).[1] Mr. and Mrs. Krapf had four children and they enjoyed a relatively comfortable living. As a young boy growing up in a country farm, Krapf recalled many escapes from death. Among them, he recalls falling in the mill stream and accidents with firearms or falling from trees as he hunted for birds' nests. As a child, he also recalled having a sensitive heart and his brushes with death would direct his mind toward spiritual matters. He would often vow secretly to lead a more holy life but found that good intentions were soon choked by the frivolity and vanity of life.

When he was eleven years old, young Krapf was severely beaten by a neighbour as chastisement for something he did not do. He does not identify the injury, but the beating left him seriously ill for six months and he was confined to his home. It was at this time that he developed an uncommon seriousness and, he said, "Left to myself my thoughts dwelt much upon eternity; and the reading of the Bible and devotional books became my delight."[2] He developed a particular attraction to the stories of the Old Testament and was especially excited by how Abraham and the Patriarchs could converse with their Creator and he hoped one day that he could also talk to God in this way. His mastery of

---

[1] P. J. L. Frankl, "Johann Ludwig Krapf and the Birth of Swahili Studies," *Zeitschrift Der Deutschen Morgenländischen Gesellschaft* 142, no. 1 (1992): 12–20. Accessed October 3, 2020. http://www.jstor.org/stable/43379871.

[2] J. Louis Krapf, *Travels, researches and missionary labors, during an eighteen year's residence in Eastern Africa* (Boston: Ticknor and Fields, 1860), 4.

these Old Testament stories meant that when he recovered from his illness and joined the workers at harvest time, he would recount the stories so vividly and earnestly that many were convinced he would one day be a minister. Although further education was limited beyond the village school for a farmer's family, young Krapf was given the opportunity to study at a grammar-school in Tübingen. This came about when his sister, on an errand to Tübingen, arrived at a wrong address and became acquainted with a kindly widow. In the conversation that ensued the widow offered Krapf a place at the school and thought that he could also tutor her son in arithmetic and perhaps continue on to study for the Church. Excited by the prospect of an education for his son, Mr. Krapf brought him to Tübingen to meet the rector in charge of the school, hoping that one day his son would be a lawyer or perhaps a clergyman.

Krapf could see later how the events of his childhood were connected by a "providential guidance": the beating from his neighbour, his sister's "mistaking the house" in Tübingen, and the opportunity for a grammar school education. During his six-months of illness, Krapf had not only mastered many of the stories of the Old Testament, but he had also begun to learn Latin. When Mr. Kaufmann, the rector, handed him a Latin grammar primer to see how familiar he was with the characters, he was pleased with Krapf's performance and promised him a place in the school.

His father, recognising the opportunity, bought the necessary books before they left Tübingen that same day. The following morning, Krapf was up at three to learn his Latin declensions and arrived at the school before eight, with a "bottle of sweet must and a hunch of bread." The "shame" of sitting in school with younger boys, already much more advanced, gave Krapf the needed encouragement to be more earnest in his studies. He took advantage of the long walks between Tübingen and Derendingen to work on his memorisation and, within six months, he found himself at the head of the class. Krapf's abilities in languages soon became evident, and he excelled in each level of classes, climbing quickly through Latin and Greek studies.

But something was missing. Krapf's early resolutions to lead a holy life were smothered by vain ambition, and although outwardly successful in his studies, he was inwardly unsettled and struggling. His journeys between Tübingen and Derendingen became memorable now, not for memory work, but for the sense of the obscured countenance of God, the vanity of self-love and ambition, and the lack of joy and peace. He longed to converse with God as the characters he had met in the Old Testament conversed with God.

His dad had given him an atlas when he first went to school, and he found himself increasingly interested in places like Somalia and Ethiopia where there were large swaths of land with so few place names, which appeared as "weißen Flecken auf der landkarte" (white spots on the map).[3] This curiosity deepened as time passed and expanded to an interest in geography and a desire to travel. He set his heart on being a "captain of a ship and to visit foreign lands," which did not sit well with his family or his father. His mother and his sister, however, who seemed to have had some influence in the home, were favourable. Finding himself outnumbered, Krapf's father graciously acquiesced but later discovered that the preparation for becoming a ship's captain was beyond their means. Krapf gave up on the dream and continued his studies, adding French and Italian to his curriculum. He was not interested in studying law, as his father had suggested at the beginning; he was not against theology but he "dreaded the learning of Hebrew, with its repulsive-looking characters and unfamiliar sounds."[4]

---

[3] Jochen Eber, *Johann Ludwig Krapf: Ein schwäbischer pionier in Ostafrika* (Basel: ArteMedia, 2006), 15.

[4] Krapf, *Travels*, 8.

Another seemingly unimportant circumstance in Krapf's life, when he was fifteen years old, became a turning point and helped to fix his future career. The rector of the school read an essay to the class on the spread of Christianity among the heathen. Thirty-three years prior, William Carey had published his "Inquiry" in England and became the father of modern missions, but Krapf had never heard of foreign missions. Also, at Basel, not far away, the first seminary dedicated to missionary training was established in 1815. The Rev. Christian Gottlieb Blumhardt (1779–1838), who was previously the Krapf family minister, was the Director. Krapf's lack of knowledge in missions, therefore, may indicate how uninvolved his father was in the life of the church.

This essay on foreign missions grabbed Krapf's attention, and the idea of being a missionary began to form in his mind. The thought of being a missionary linked well with his desire to travel and his interest in geography, but as time progressed, he could not escape from the Parable of the Sower. "How," he thought, "can I take the gospel to the heathen when the gospel has fallen on my own heart as on stony ground?"[5] The lack of a true spiritual experience and a prepared heart troubled him and drove him to read the Bible more earnestly and to pray that the Lord would open up his understanding and give him a "quickening knowledge of it."[6]

As the Easter holidays approached in 1825, he recorded that on the walk home from Tübingen, the thought came to him, he said, "with the force of a command," to go to the church Missionary Inspector (Director) in Basel to announce that he was willing to give himself to missions. The idea garnered a mixed response from his family. His mother and sister, again, supported him. With a letter of introduction from his mother, fifteen-year-old Krapf headed out towards Basel for the Missionary Institute of what was then known as the German Missionary Society.

---

[5] Krapf, *Travels*, 9.
[6] Krapf, *Travels*, 9.

The inspector kindly recognised the boy's youthful zeal, but he was concerned about his unpreparedness, because he was too young to attend the school and also because he believed that young Krapf did not know true Christian conversion. The inspector graciously advised Krapf to continue his studies, cultivate Christian friends in his neighbourhood and search after a knowledge of the gospel in his own heart. He also gave him permission to remain there that night and to spend a week at the Missionary Institute. It was there, Krapf testified, that he first met true Christians who, on their knees, prayed with him, and through these acquaintances, Krapf experienced true evangelical conversion.

Krapf returned home determined to become a missionary. He gave himself privately to the study of Hebrew, which he had so much feared, and in one year, his fifth and final year at the grammar school, he had read the greater part of the Old Testament in the original language. He also followed the advice of the Rev. Blumhardt who had encouraged him to seek out Christian friends. Krapf does not recount the details of his conversion experience. However, as a result of Rev. Blumhardt's advice, during that year, he realised the importance of Christian company and became convinced that "a Christian can only be formed amongst Christians."[7] It is amongst them [older Christians]," he wrote, "that a young Christian first becomes conscious of his own spiritual wants by witnessing the faith, patience, and constancy of aged persons in the various trials of life."

[7] Krapf, *Travels*, 10.

Chapter 2
Years of Severe and Painful Struggle

In 1827, at seventeen years old, Krapf finished his grammar school education and had set his heart on becoming a missionary. Rev. Blumhardt had not forgotten his visit at Easter two years previously and Krapf was filled with "inexpressible joy"[11] when he received an invitation to the Basel Mission school. Rev. Blumhardt was satisfied that he had truly experienced conversion. Again, his father's opposition may give us a window into the spiritual life of the man, but his mother appears to be more spiritually alert. His father opposed this choice because he was afraid of him "being buried alive in a foreign land."[1] But Krapf was determined and, with the backing of his mother and sister again, his father was finally convinced and accompanied him to Basel to begin his studies.

Missionary interest in Basel predated Carey and the Baptism Missionary Society in England. The rise of German Piety and the Moravian Herrnhut Community gave expression to a number of Christian attributes associated with Pietism, including the necessity of personal regeneration, the importance of the Bible and devotional literature in the transformation of the inner man, and his subsequent way of life. In the mid-18th century, Basel began to emerge as an international Pietist centre, principally because of its proximity both to Switzerland and to German Pietism in Württemberg. In 1780 a group of Pietists formed the German Christian Society as an international network for mutual encouragement and for the promotion of Pietism. A monthly publication followed, *"Gatherings for Lovers of Christian Truth,"* as a collection

---

[1] J. Louis Krapf, *Travels, researches and missionary labors, during an eighteen year's residence in Eastern Africa* (Boston: Ticknor and Fields, 1860), 10.

13

of excerpts gathered from various reports of the members, for the promotion of Christian instruction, apologetics and foreign missions.[2]

The Basel Missionary Training Institute, generally known as the Basel Mission, was established in 1815, by Blumhardt and Christian Friedrich Spittler (1782–1867) who had been involved in the Christian Society. It was a non-confessional, non-denominational school and the first school established solely for the purpose of training missionaries.

Krapf entered the Basel college as an impressionable and impulsive young man. He would look back at those years of training as "years of severe and painful struggle," when he was being "purified by fire."[3] It was not the learning that he found difficult as much as finding his own identity. First, he found the rules of the school to be quite severe, especially in prohibiting the reading of the so-called mystics. Whether it was this prohibition or his "excited imagination," but, within two years, he had made "a stealthy acquaintance with the forbidden writings of such mystics as Madame Guyon and Jacob Behmen,"[4] and had imbibed, as he said, the "pernicious doctrines" of these mystics. Indeed, he was so influenced by their writings that he abandoned the college and his missionary vision and returned home to give himself to honest and happy labour with his hands. His parents were understandably upset with the waste of their financial outlay. But their pride also took a hit, for, having been brought up to such a level of education, Krapf would be a disgrace to the whole family if he "were to sink again to the level of a mere tiller of the soil."[5]

---

[2] For a discussion on the "spiritual roots" of Krapf and his missionary partner Johannes Rebmann, see: Steven Paas, *Johannes Rebmann: A servant of God in Africa before the rise of Western colonialism* (Oregon: Wipf & Stock, 2018), 25–39.

[3] Krapf, *Travels*, 11.

[4] Krapf, *Travels*, 11.

[5] Krapf, *Travels*, 11.

Either convinced or cajoled, Krapf returned to Basel to complete his course and was subsequently ordained to the ministry of the Lutheran Church. But the thought of the foreign mission field would not leave him. He cousin, with the same name, entered the college and Krapf's sense of calling to the mission field intensified. He consoled himself with the argument that he could do in his homeland what his cousin intended to do in foreign lands. But the shallow comfort he found in this reasoning betrayed the rationale of an uncertain and struggling mind. Wrestling with the plight of the heathen, Krapf accepted a call to a church in Wolfenhausen, in central Germany. Even here, though, he could not escape the call of the heathen. Everywhere he turned he was faced with the reality of those who had never heard the gospel. In a letter dated 1835, he wrote,

> The inducements to mission work appear to me in a new light. In the needs of my congregation, I recognized those of non-Christians in a measure which affected me very deeply; in their sorrow I recognized the wretchedness of the heathen; the cry for help from my own congregation seemed an echo from heathen lands. The grace which I myself enjoyed, and which I commended to my own people was, I felt, for the heathen as well, but there may be no one to proclaim it to them. In this country everyone may without difficulty find the way to life; in those lands there may be no one to show the way. Here, in almost every house the Holy Scriptures may be found; there, the Scriptures are only scantily distributed. This seems to me a powerful incentive to think seriously of missionary work.[6]

1836 was a watershed year. In that year, as he resisted the call of the foreign mission-field, Krapf was faced with another trial

---

[6] Paul E. Kretzmann, *The Life of Ludwig Krapf: The Missionary Explorer of East Africa* (Columbus, Ohio: The Book Concern, n.d.), 31–32.

concerning a sermon he had preached in which he promoted a particularly radical position on the end of the world. The Consistory objected to his sermon and Krapf resigned. His plan was to return home and work as a private tutor. However, around that time, he was reacquainted with an old friend from his days at the Basel college, Peter Fjelstädt, a Swede, who had just returned from Smyrna where he was serving with the CMS.

No doubt, Krapf had heard of the CMS, for this organisation was an outlet for many of the Basel-trained missionaries. The CMS was established in 1799 as a mission of evangelical Anglicanism. In the first fifty years (1799–1849), however, while the CMS had a potential world-wide influence throughout the British Empire, it struggled to recruit missionaries in England, and during those years the mission focused on literary and translation work.[7] With difficulty engaging English missionaries, the CMS looked to Europe, particularly, German Lutherans who did not have the missionary outlet to match their zeal. The partnership between the CMS and The Basel Mission, therefore, was mutually beneficial, and the Basel Mission became the main recruiting seminary, even after 1825 when the CMS opened its own seminary in Islington, England.

Fjelstädt had been a close friend with Krapf back in 1829 while they were in Basel. Now realizing his friend's struggle, Fjelstädt encouraged Krapf to rethink his position and give himself again to the work of foreign missions. "I took time to reflect," Krapf wrote, "called prayer to my aid and arrived at the joyful conviction that I ought again to dedicate myself to the service of missions and find in the starting point of my career its goal and resting-place." His missionary impulse was reignited and Krapf applied to the work of the CMS with the intention of going to Smyrna with Fjelstädt. He took up learning Turkish and modern Greek but was

---

[7] Eugene Stock, *One Hundred Years: Being the Short History of the Church Missionary Society* (London: Church Missionary Society, 1899), 19.

informed that at that time (early 1836) there were no positions available with the mission, but that he should apply to the Mission at Basel and wait for further orders. And so, in 1836, Krapf returned to the mission college in Basel and waited for a posting with the CMS.

In the autumn of that year, Mr. Dandeson Coates, the Lay Secretary of the CMS (1824–1846) was in Basel on behalf of the mission and Krapf had the opportunity to meet with him. At that time also, a missionary on his way to Ethiopia had died suddenly in Cairo and Krapf was asked to take his place. It was this region of Africa that had initially interested Krapf. He immediately switched his language studies from Turkish and Modern Greek to Ethiopic and Amharic.

It had been ten years since Krapf had entered the college at Basel and, clearly, those years proved difficult. He looked back on that period of his life as a time of testing and purifying. Finally, after much uncertainty and distraction of mind, Krapf was restored to his "former healthy tone of mind" and from the "doubts that had so long threatened [his] peace." On February 6, 1837, he set out on the long and difficult journey to Ethiopia, via Marseille, Malta, and finally landing on the African continent at Alexandria, Egypt sometime in April. He travelled on to Cairo, much of the way by boat on the Nile, where he remained until September. The time spent at Cairo with other CMS missionaries gave him time to prepare the next leg of his journey and to learn colloquial Arabic.

Continuing on from Cairo, the journey brought him to Suez by camel as there was neither road nor railway, and from Suez he sailed to Jidda on an Arabian vessel. From Jidda, he travelled twenty-two days by boat to Massowa, modern-day Mitsiwa, Eretria, but at that time a major Ethiopian seaport and landing point.

A Young Ludwig Krapf

Chapter 3
Ethiopia and the Orthodox Church

The CMS missionary effort in Ethiopia was part of the "Mediterranean Mission" focused on the Eastern Orthodox Church and,
particularly, the Coptic Church of Egypt. Interest in North Africa
began to move towards Ethiopia in 1817 with the unexpected discovery of some manuscripts of the Ethiopic Scriptures. The CMS
then commissioned Rev. Samuel Lee (1783–1852), an expert in
Oriental studies, to research the Orthodox Church in Ethiopia. In
his report, Lee concluded that of all the expressions of Eastern Or-
thodoxy, the Ethiopian Church was "the most corrupt and super-
stitious in the world."[1]

In 1830, the CMS sent Rev. Samuel Gobat (1799–1879), a
Swiss Calvinist, to establish a mission in the northern part of Ethiopia. The basis of operations at that time was not to establish
Protestant communities, but to attempt a reform within the exist-
ing Church, "raising her from the dust, by imparting to her the
light of gospel truth."[2] The hope was that by influencing the Orthodox church and reforming it, then that church, in turn, would
"hold forth the same light to the surrounding heathen."[3] It was an
optimistic plan and early attempts seemed to have some success,
at least in outward acceptance. Gobat was known for his "ener-
getic practicality and consummate Christian diplomacy," and he
was able to relate well with the people and was well received with

---

[1] Eugene Stock, *One Hundred Years: Being the Short History of the Church Missionary Society* (London: Church Missionary Society, 1899), 55.
[2] Eugene Stock, *The missionary career of Dr. Krapf* (London: Church Missionary
Society, 1882), 5.
[3] Stock, *The missionary career of Dr. Krapf*, 6.

the Orthodox Church.[4] However, Gobat retired from Ethiopia in December 1832, because of ill health and, although he attempted to return in 1835, ill health again forced him back to Europe.[5] Others went to replace him, namely Rev. Karl Wilhelm Isenberg (1806–1864) who had worked directly with Gobat and later Rev. Carl Heinrich Blumhardt.

When Krapf arrived in Ethiopia then, the "land of [his] youthful dreams and aspirations,"[6] in December 1837, he joined Isenberg and Blumhardt. He was one month short of his twenty-eighth birthday. Given his attentiveness in language study, his love of travel and geographical literature and his diligence in preparation for the field, there is no doubt that he had brought with him a copy of the *Journal of Three Years Residence in Abyssinia* published by Samuel Gobat in 1834. This book included "A Brief History of the Church of Abyssinia," by Samuel Lee. At any rate, it is evident from his subsequent literary achievements that Krapf was well informed in the geography, ethnography, topography and religious make-up of Ethiopia.

When Krapf arrived at Massowa, then, there was some necessary paperwork to complete; a custom, he says, of meeting Ubié, the Chief, presenting a gift and obtaining a grant to travel through his dominion. His money was carefully counted and his luggage and the luggage of other travelers arriving from Germany was scrutinized for fear that they were bringing in weapons.[7] With the formalities over and with a grant of four soldiers to escort him, he

---

[4] Jonathan J. Bonk, "Gobat, Samuel," *Biographical Dictionary of Christian Missions*, ed. Gerald H. Anderson (New York: Macmillan Reference USA, 1998), 245.

[5] Samuel Lee, "A brief history of the church of Abyssinia" *Journal of three years residence in Abyssinia* by Samuel Gobat (London: Hatchard and Son, and Seeley and Sons, 1834), 332.

[6] J. Louis Krapf, *Travels, researches and missionary labors, during an eighteen year's residence in Eastern Africa* (Boston: Ticknor and Fields, 1860), 12.

[7] H. Gundert, *Biography of Rev. Charles Isenberg: missionary of the Church Missionary Society to Abyssinia and Western India from 1832 to 1864,* Trans. C. & M. Isenberg (London: Church Missionary Society, 1885), 28.

set out for Adowa (variously spelt *Adoa, Adowah*), the capital of Tigray (also spelt *Tigré*), about 270 kilometers south. Getting his baggage transported to the mission station also proved difficult; the experience, he said, "initiated him into the mysteries of African travel." He had hired thirty-one oxen to carry his goods to the mission station, 6000 ft. above sea level. When he realised, however, that the porters were attempting to take advantage of him, he refused to pay, and an altercation ensued.

In a strategic ploy, the porters withdrew to the mountains, reckoning that in Krapf's helplessness he would give in to their demands. He refused, and after three days, they descended the mountain again and positioned themselves for battle a hundred paces from the missionaries' tents. A couple of shots in the air from Krapf gave them pause, but just as the situation began to escalate, his fellow missionary Wilhelm Isenberg appeared with sixty helpers to escort him back to Adowa.

Before they had reached the mission station at Adowa, they encountered more obstructions from those who opposed protestant missionaries, a forecast of what was ahead. The three men then (Isenberg, Blumhardt, and Krapf) began with some public relations and a visit to the Prince of Tigray; they were well received and promised protection from the prince. But such promises were no protection against the hatred stirred up by the two French Roman Catholic priests, Arnaud d'Abbadie and Giuseppe Sapeto, who had stirred up trouble burning Bibles that were distributed. They had also convinced the chief that only the Roman Catholic Church could work with the Ethiopians because they were more closely related. In addition to this, Isenberg, the senior missionary, had begun to build a new house and with the necessary excavation for foundations and building material, the enemies of the mission circulated rumours that they were digging a tunnel for English soldiers to come and conquer Ethiopia. Krapf, scarcely on the field two months, and his missionary colleagues,

was summoned before the Chief Priest and told that Ubié's patience "is exhausted; he can no longer suffer in the country people
of a different creed and religious agitators."[8] It was revealed later
that the Roman Catholic priests had bought this opposition from
the local Orthodox priests for the price of fifteen pounds. Ubié
stated that he had no personal antipathy against the missionaries
but that he was unable to protect them any longer from the slan-
ders of their enemies.[9]

The three retreated to Massowa and waited for orders from the
mission. The work in Northern Ethiopia that Gobat had established in 1830 collapsed. Isenberg and Blumhardt returned to
Cairo. Krapf, however, still fresh with zeal, was not so easily
moved and began developing his own plans to move further inland to Shewa (variously spelled, *Shoa*), an area surrounding the
modern city of Addis Ababa. This area was ruled by an absolute
monarch, Sahela Selassie and was, for the most part, Orthodox
Christian, an expression of the Egyptian Coptic Church. In the
east, towards the coast, there were a number of Islamists and to
the south "tribes of heathen Oromo."[10] Krapf's mind was directed
towards this people group known as the Oromo.[11]

His first thought was to enter through the Somali coast but was
informed that this would not be possible. He set sail for Mokha,
on the other side of the Red Sea, where he learned that the best
landing place for Shewa was Tajurra (Tagurrä or modern day
Tadjoura, Djibouti), further south towards the Gulf of Aden. Before he could sail further south, however, he was taken ill with
dysentery and forced to return to Cairo, arriving on September
27, 1838.

---

[8] Gundert, *Isenberg*, 28.
[9] Gundert, *Isenberg*, 28.
[10] Krapf, *Travels*, 31.
[11] Krapf referred to this people group as the Galla, or Gallas people. They are, however, known as the Oromo and I will use this term throughout.

Chapter 4
Ethiopia and the Struggle for the Oromo

In the spring of 1839, one year after he had first been expelled from Ethiopia, Krapf sailed into the bay at Tadjoura, in an attempt to circumnavigate the opposition at Adowa. He was accompanied on the journey by his friend and more senior colleague, Isenberg, who had previously received an invitation from the king, Sahela Selassie, to come to his kingdom. Coastal East Africa at this time was dominated and ruled by the Arabs, and permission was granted by the Sultan to enter. After four weeks of negotiations on the cost of transport, they set out for Shewa on April 27. The journey was difficult, travelling by camel, in the style of the Arabs, Krapf wrote, "suffering from lack of water and heat exhaustion, the temperatures rising as high as 110 °F."[1] There were few people and "besides gazelles and ostriches there were few wild animals." At one point, however, they encountered a herd of elephants, of which, he said, the "camels are dreadfully afraid." They reached Ankober safely on June 3, 1839, and after some days waiting for permission from the king to proceed, arrived at their final destination on June 11.

Krapf and Isenberg visited the king and were given a "very friendly reception,"[2] although they were aware that they lived there very much at his mercy. Krapf realized the king's bias against the missionaries from the beginning. The king had promised the missionaries six boys whom he could educate, but he later reneged because they could give him no assurance of craftsmen and artisans or gun-makers from Europe.

---

[1] C. Tilstone Beke, "Appendix to Messrs. Isenberg and Krapf's Journal," *Journal of the Royal Geographical Society* (London: John Murray, 1841), 10:580–586.

[2] J. Louis Krapf, *Travels, researches and missionary labors, during an eighteen year's residence in Eastern Africa* (Boston: Ticknor and Fields, 1860), 21.

The missionaries forged a working relationship with the king and continued their work as much as they could. Krapf formed a school from volunteers, boys like fourteen-year-old Guebra Georgis who had a capacity and a willingness to learn in the hope that "if his heart should be changed by the Holy Spirit, he would become very useful to our mission."[3] In the first few months of school, Isenberg writes, it was "attended by thirty to forty scholars, young and old."[4] Isenberg spent much of his time preparing his Amharic work for the press. Krapf, along with the work of the school, began to make "particular inquiries respecting everything connected with the Oromo, their religious notions, manners and customs, their geographical extension."

On August 9, 1839, Krapf wrote in his journal that he had begun to collect a vocabulary of the Oromo language. In November, six months after their arrival at Ankober, Isenberg left to prepare his Amharic work for publishing in London. Krapf wept that morning as his friend and co-worker left, knowing that he was alone, but he was comforted by the words of the Saviour, "I am with you always."[5] The absence of Isenberg, however, and the severe loneliness provided the proper environment for him to give himself to the work, particularly the study of the Oromo language.

---

[3] Ludwig Krapf, *Journals of the Rev. Messrs. Isenberg and Krapf, missionaries of the Church Missionary Society* (London: Church Missionary Society, 1843), 84.

[4] C.W. Isenberg, "A few remarks concerning the nation of the Gallas, and an evangelical mission among them," *An imperfect outline of the elements of the Galla language* by J. Ludwig Krapf (London: Church Missionary Society, 1840), xii.

[5] In his autobiography Krapf mentions a French traveler who arrived shortly before Isenberg left. How long he stayed or with whom he stayed is not known, but Krapf found him to be untruthful and untrustworthy in the reports regarding geographical discoveries and despite Krapf's kindness, he incited the king against Krapf and also published material that Krapf had given him without citing Krapf as the source. "Alas!" Krapf wrote, "such unconscientious statements are too common on the part of travellers, who huddle up a book and obtain honors and emoluments at the expense of geographical truth." We know also that another traveler, Charles Tilstone Beke, a traveller and biblical critic, was in the region, writing for the Royal Geographical Association. See *Journal of the Royal Geographical Society* (London: John Murray, 1841) 10:455–468, 469–488, 580–586. Apart from these hostile Europeans, Krapf was alone for most of his time in Ankober.

During this time, he records in his journals, he had many conversations on religious subjects with the Orthodox priests.

Krapf's focus, however, was beginning to shift from the Orthodox Church. He could see that the differences were too great and the points of contention too many. He could see also an opportunity to reach the heart of Africa through Oromo territory, and, in time, he would influence the entire CMS operations in East Africa. This change of focus freed Krapf from confrontation with the Orthodox Christians and, over time, he formed a friendly relationship with them. He even writes of attending the Orthodox Church on the Lord's Day.

He also formed a very public friendship with the king, but this friendship came at the price. Krapf was somewhat obligated to the whims of the king; he was ordered, for example, to accompany him on many military expeditions to the Oromo region from where Selassie had levied a tribute. The first of these was in January and February 1840, just two months after Isenberg had left. During these military operations, as Selassie exacted his tribute, often with military force, Krapf was gathering information, making connections, and forming friendships. He formed a friendship, for example, with the son of Queen Tshāmē, of the Oromo tribe Moolofallada. The queen's son expressed a desire to learn from Krapf if the King of Shewa would allow it. Krapf was also locating possible mission stations on these military journeys with the king and had identified Mt. Yerer and another location, both south of present-day Addis Ababa, and the third at Muger to the north, not far from the Blue Nile.

Krapf was also influential in forging relations between Ethiopia and Britain and with the British diplomat, William Cornwallis Harris. Harris had been sent from Aden with presents and a draft treaty for the abolition of slavery. Despite the friendship, however, and the benefit of an alliance forged with England, Krapf was not surprised at the vicissitudes that characterized his friendship with

Selassie. Although he was good natured and possessed a sense of justice, and many good qualities,[6] Selassie was also too influenced by the priests and his chiefs and "the desire for personal enrichment, and the Oriental habit of accumulating dead treasures."[7] He was also interested in foreign technology and craftsmen and professionals—doctors, masons, smiths etc. Selassie was indeed influenced towards a dislike for protestant missionaries by the "bigoted priests and monks who tried to inspire the king with a distrust of foreigners."[8] The bias came to the surface again when, in translating the Oromo, Krapf used the Roman alphabet rather than the Semitic Ethiopic (Ge-ez) characters, which did not sit well with the king.

At the beginning of the 1842, Krapf was physically and mentally at the end of his strength. With three years of hard labouring, however, Krapf could see the fruit of his ministry at Ankober, and he had no reason to think this would be obstructed if he could maintain his friendship with the king. He had distributed 1000 copies of the Scriptures and "many of the priests of [Shewa] had been awakened to a knowledge of the truth, and to a consciousness of the corrupt state of their church."[9] His little school of ten boys whom he fed, clothed and educated at home was prospering, and the king had presented him with a silver sword, which conferred on him the rank of a governor. He had also accomplished much in his studies of the Oromo language, with translations of the Gospels of Matthew and John, as well as the first grammar and vocabulary in that language published at that time.

However, he had also come to the conclusion that his work in Shewa was unnecessarily limited. He could not carry it alone and having seen the vagaries of Ethiopian Christianity, he was not

---

[6] Krapf, *Travels*, 28.
[7] Krapf, *Travels*, 28.
[8] Krapf, *Travels*, 26.
[9] Krapf, *Travels*, 71.

convinced the mission strategy of the CMS was a wise one. Although they had given him the reins, so-to-speak, as far as the local operations were concerned, there needed to be a definite strategy developed for the interior and sufficient funds in order to enable them to carry out the work. It was well known that the Society had struggled to maintain the necessary funding for their operation. In 1840, Isenberg made a plea through the Society for the "Missionary public ... to increase its liberality towards the Society's general funds, in order to enable them to send that support to [Shewa] which is necessary to continue the mission there."[10]

As far back as 1838,[11] a plan had begun to form in Krapf's mind. It formed the early stages of an elaborate and effective missionary strategy which focused on the Oromo people whom he believed to be "the most intellectual people in eastern Africa."[12] They had not been influenced by Islam nor bound by this ancient form of Eastern Christianity, nor had they developed any relation with Europeans which was corrupting the coastal tribes and thwarting the gospel effort. He was concerned also that Islam would make progress in converting the Oromo, which would be, he said "a strong bulwark against the introduction of Christianity and true morality into Africa." [13]

Krapf believed that if he could penetrate the region to the south, their numbers were so great, that they might be the most effective method for the evangelisation of Africa. His vision for the Oromo people was built around his understanding of the Reformation in Germany. In the providence of God, Germany had been used to give the world a pure gospel in the 16th century, so Krapf believed the Oromo, who make up such a large portion of East Africa, would be used to bring the gospel to Central Africa.

---

[10] Isenberg, *A few remarks*, xiii.

[11] Krapf, *Travels*, 90.

[12] M. Louise Pirouet, "The legacy of Johann Ludwig Krapf," *International bulletin of missionary research*, No. 2 (April 1, 1999): 23, 70.

[13] Krapf, *Travels*, 101.

He often referred to this region as "Ormania" analogous, he thought, to "Germania."[14] "To my mind," he said "Ormania is the Germany of Africa." "Give us the Oromo, and Central Africa is ours."[15]

The problem that he faced, however, was getting to the Oromo people through the mission at Shewa. He knew he needed to move further inland and live among them, but some of the Oromo people had rebelled against King Selassie, which had created a hostile situation and made the roads unsafe to travel.

Another problem emerged at this time. Although he had established himself in Shewa and was friendly with the king, there was no guarantee that others would be given access to the kingdom to help the mission. This became clear early in 1842 when word reached him that two fellow missionaries, Müller and J.J. Mühleisen (also known as Mühleisen-Arnold in later years), had reached the coast at Tadjoura and found it difficult to get through. Krapf decided to meet the two new missionaries at the coast, take a furlough to Egypt and marry Fraülein Dietrich, with whom he had been corresponding.

On March 10, 1842, Krapf set out for the coast. He decided to hike north, through the Ethiopian highlands, and reach the coast at Massawa, rather than the much easier and direct route east to Tadjoura. As difficult as this would be—and he knew the difficulties—he had reason for taking this route. First, he wanted to meet the new Archbishop of Abuna and ascertain his sentiments towards Protestant missionaries. Second, he wanted to see what the situation was in Adowa since they were expelled in 1838 and discover if it was possible to reestablish the mission there. A third reason was to open up a new route in case the way from Tadjoura

---

[14] Wolbert Smidt, "A remarkable chapter of German research history: the Protestant mission and the Oromo in the nineteenth century" *Cultural Research in Northeastern Africa: German Histories and Stories* (Frankfurt: Frobenius-Institut: Addis Ababa: Goethe-Institut; Mekelle: Mekelle University, 2015), 60–77.

[15] Krapf, *Travels*, 101.

had been completely closed. The lengthy diary entries for this period between leaving Ankober and reaching Massawa make alarming and thrilling reading, the kind that would have sold well during that period of imperial expansion in Africa, when "travelogues" were popular reading material.

Krapf had read these travelogues himself as a young boy, but now he found himself writing of the most harrowing experiences of enemy attacks, robberies, dangerous mountainous terrain, wild beasts, and oppressive temperatures. On this particular journey, he was betrayed and taken captive. "What would our friends at home feel," he wrote,

> if they could know for a moment the dangers, difficulties, sorrows, and privations, in which a Missionary abroad is sometimes placed ... How miserable should I have been, if I had not known the fire-pillar, the almighty covenant-God, accompanying me with His invisible presence.[16]

Mentally and emotionally exhausted, barefoot, lame and fatigued from the trek—having been robbed of everything but a few shillings, his papers and left with his worst donkey—Krapf arrived at the coast on May 4, 1842. Letters home to Mr. Hoffman at the Basel Mission indicate the reduced state of his emotional and spiritual energies.[17] He was further disappointed that his friends, who had come to strengthen the mission at Shewa, had returned to Cairo, not having been promised safe passage to Ankober.

---

[16] Krapf, *Journals*, 334–335, 340.
[17] von Walter Buder, "Rosine Krapf und Pauline Flad: Zwei Frauen erleben Äthiopien in unruhiger Zeit," in *Kirche und Schule in Äthiopien* (Heidelberg: TABOR SOCIETY) Heft 60 / November 2007, 17.

Chapter 5
Fraülein Dietrich and the Search
for the Oromo

For the past three years—between 1838 and 1842—Krapf had been alone, facing difficulties and disappointments, wrestling with the possibility of reaching the Oromo people and struggling with the Society on how best to prosecute that effort. Of all the CMS missionaries who had laboured in Ethiopia, Krapf had spent more time there than any of them. Experience had "convinced [him] that an unmarried missionary could not eventually prosper."[1] Now at the coast for the first time in three years, he had arranged a number of endeavours to make this trip as efficient as possible in the hope of returning more prepared to resume the work at Shewa.

He sailed from Massowa to Aden and from Aden he obtained free passage to Suez from Major Cornwallis Harris, the British Consul whom he had helped in connection with the king of Shewa. His final destination was Alexandria where he had planned to meet Fraülein Rosine Dietrich and marry her. While he had never met her, he had heard of Fraülein Dietrich and had been enquiring about her from the secretary of the Society. It would be wrong to suggest that Krapf had "cold-bloodedly decided that he needed a wife," or that there was little romance in the marriage.[2] There was more to Krapf's marriage than mere physical desire or convenience; it was a marriage of the minds. Rosine had been engaged to a Mr. Köhnlein who was a friend of Krapf's. In 1837, while Krapf was on his way to Ethiopia and

---

[1] Krapf, *Travels*, 72.
[2] R.C. Bridges, "Introduction to the Second Edition," *Travels, Researches and Missionary Labors, During an Eighteen Year's residence in Eastern Africa*, Rprt. 1860 (London: Routledge, 1968), 14.

Köhnlein on his way to Algeria, their paths crossed in Marseille. Unfortunately, Köhnlein became ill and died in Marseille, and Krapf asked for his friend's estate.

Among the private papers, Krapf found letters from his friend's fiancée, Fraülein Dietrich, and he was so impressed by the content of her letters that she remained on his mind.[3]

So, from Ethiopia, having felt that the work there would be better accomplished with a wife, he inquired from the Inspector of the mission, Mr. Hoffmann, whom he trusted. Mr. Hoffmann recommended her for marriage. Convinced that Rosine was both devout and courageous, Krapf wrote to her, explaining his circumstances and asked her to marry him, with a view to joining him at Shewa. She agreed and they arranged to meet in Alexandria, where they were married on September 22, 1842. He was thirty-two and she was twenty-five.

Rosine Dietrich was born on July 19, 1817 in Basel.[4] Her father was born in Alsace, France, close to the German border, and in addition to her elementary education, she was fluent in French. From childhood, it appears, she had been keen on missionary work and her desire especially was to be a teacher for young girls. Her letters, many of them written in French, reveal a thoughtful and spiritual woman. She also indicates her desire for a husband who would strengthen her for the cause of Christ, "for the nations that have plunged into the darkness of paganism, Mohammedanism and a fallen Christianity."[5] The marriage between Krapf and Rosine, therefore, was by all accounts a happy marriage, although they were both very clear, from the beginning, that the purpose of their marriage bond was specifically for Christian service.

---

[3] von Walter Buder, "Rosine Krapf und Pauline Flad: Zwei Frauen erleben Äthiopien in unruhiger Zeit," in *Kirche und Schule in Äthiopien*, (Heidelberg: TABOR SOCIETY) Heft 60 / November 2007, 17

[4] E. C. Dawson, "Mrs. Krapf in East Africa" *Missionary Heroines of the Cross*, (London: Seeley, Service & Co. Limited, 1933), 175-179.

[5] von Walter Buder, "Rosine Krapf," 17.

Mr. and Mrs. Krapf left Egypt soon after the wedding and arrived in Tadjoura on November 20, 1842, accompanied by his friends Isenberg and Mühleisen. When they arrived at Tadjoura, they were informed by the Sultan that the King of Shewa had denied access to all Europeans. Isenberg and Mühleisen decided that they would go back north and try to approach the Oromo from the west, trekking further out towards Gondar. Although the CMS Committee in London was not yet convinced, Krapf still believed the only way to reach the Oromo people was from the Swahili Coast. However, he was willing to attempt passage one last time through Massowa, so he and his wife sailed north again to rejoin Isenberg and Mühleisen who had already begun the trek inland towards the Tigray region.

Navigating the western shore of the Red Sea in a small and rugged Arab sailing dhow was uncomfortable and dangerous. Rosine wrote from Massowa on May 15, 1843, describing the voyage. She was the only woman on the small wooden craft with little moving space. Accommodating the working crew amid the swells was difficult, and on the last days of the journey the small party ran out of drinking water. In her letters home, however, Rosine downplayed the dangers and hardships and spoke more of the view and the splendor of the Ethiopian mountains as they sailed up the coast. She showed great sympathy and a love for the people, describing their looks and their clothes, their hospitality, and their food. One historian writes, "you feel reading them that she loves people, even those who follow the teaching of the false prophet ... this kind sympathy is embedded in a remarkable mind and heart, and in a firm trust in God."[6]

When the Krapfs arrived at Massowa, they were informed that they could not pass through the Gondar region on the west. The British had an ambassador in the region also, and he too was at

---

[6] von Walter Buder, "Rosine Krapf," 18.

the point of leaving because of the level of distrust against the Europeans. Krapf wrote to the king indicating his desire to come, but the letter stirred up powerful agitation in the Orthodox Church. Meetings were held in all the churches of the capital, and deputations of priests and monks were dispatched to the palace to implore his Majesty that the missionaries might not be readmitted. "Their works," said the Orthodox priests, "are not ours, and their book is different from ours. If they are suffered to return, the people will fall away from the faith of their fathers." [7] The British Ambassador pleaded with the king on behalf of the missionaries, but to no avail. "Isenberg and Krapf cannot come again to my country," he said,

> My people will not allow them. I have considered upon this subject for a long time, and it is better that they remain away. I will not permit either to come again beyond the Hawash ... The Chief of the road will stop them, and take their property if they attempt the journey, and perhaps kill them.

Despite having signed a treaty with Queen Victoria, pledging that British travelers would have free access, the king of Shewa broke his treaty and refused entry. It seemed that every way was blocked. "How mysterious and marvelous are the Lord's ways," Krapf wrote,

> When we fully believe that a door of great and successful activity has been opened, He closes it before our eyes, and changes our joy into weeping and sorrow. But nevertheless, He is, and remains, our faithful Lord, whether He makes us to rejoice or weep. With Him we will stand or fall, as He pleases. He humiliates us, but He will lift us up again when

---

[7] J.L. Krapf, "Missionary Openings in East Africa," *The Church Missionary Intelligencer, A Monthly Journal of Missionary Information,* ed. Eugene Stock (London: Seeleys, Hatchard and J. Nisbet & Co, 1850), 1:387.

we have put away our confidence in human flesh and strength. Persecutions have at all times yielded rather profit to the Church of Christ, as her messengers have been purified in themselves, and, at the same time, have been compelled to proclaim the good tidings of Christ crucified to those who have not heard them before. Therefore, let us, in full confidence in the Lord's wonderful dispensation, take the bright side of the fall of our Mission in Shoa.[8]

Although Krapf could see the hand of God in the situation and took comfort in the knowledge of a sovereign God, he was not willing to concede the mission to priests and monks and the worldly rulers of Ethiopia. In his mind, he had been developing an East Coast strategy to the African interior. However, before he attempted this, his tenacious spirit would not give up on Ethiopia so easily. He said, "I did not allow myself to be daunted by the bad news which I had heard in Massowa; but proceeded with my wife through the Shoho land to the frontier of Tigray, with a large supply of Amharic and Ethiopic Bibles and Testaments."[9] The journey was difficult as they moved inland towards the Tigray to their fellow-workers, Isenberg and Mühleisen-Arnold. Rosine was pregnant with their first child and the trek into the mountains was a steep, stony and thorny trek and the porters were difficult to work with.

Along the way, on May 26, Rosine gave birth prematurely to a little girl, on a dry riverbed, "with no tent or nurse or surgeon." Krapf wrote, "In the Shoho wilderness, my beloved wife was prematurely delivered of a little daughter whom I christened 'Eneba' *a tear*. I had to bury the dear child, for she lived only a few hours, under a tree by the wayside."[10] Her husband was devastated and to add to his suffering, the Shoa porters would not wait for

[8] Krapf, *Intelligencer*, 1:387–388.
[9] Krapf, *Travels*, 90–91.
[10] Krapf, *Travels*, 91.

her to recover and there was no village where his wife could rest. Three days later they were obliged to continue, broken hearted at the loss. Rosine wrote to her mother, on June 6, after they had returned to Massowa, about the death of her child and the "blessed losses" referencing the trial of Job (1:21). She praised her husband for his assistance, and she unburdened her heart of the awful trial, lamenting at the "silent burial that can't be described but can be felt." "Yes," she continued, "tears flow, but I know where my child is and am happy."[11]

When the Krapfs arrived at the frontier of Tigray, they "busied [themselves] distributing the Bibles,"[12] which were well received. Isenberg and Mühleisen, however, informed them that access through the Tigray had been denied. Krapf was angry and frustrated at the hostility of the priesthood at Adowa and the European Catholics who were inciting it. In a letter dated August 1843, he said of them, "a more beggarly people cannot exist."[13]

The CMS was forced to abandon all efforts in Ethiopia. Isenberg and Mühleisen returned to Egypt and eventually were sent to India where they spent many years. Mühleisen distinguished himself as a scholar in Islam studies. The Krapfs, however, continued to hope that God would give the Oromo another chance, and as his wife wrote, citing again the analogy of the Protestant Reformation of the 16th century, "the time of the Reformation does not seem to have come yet and so our hopes are very low. But the matter is commended to the Lord, it is His business and not ours."[14]

In this frame of mind then—a mixture of frustration, anger, sorrow and yet dependence on a sovereign God—they arrived again at the coast and Krapf knew the time had come for him to act on his East Coast strategy. His mind had long been engaged

---

[11] von Walter Buder, "Rosine Krapf," 19
[12] Krapf, *Travels*, 61.
[13] von Walter Buder, "Rosine Krapf," 18.
[14] von Walter Buder, "Rosine Krapf," 19.

on this idea, and he had often wondered why no one had attempted the African interior through the many rivers that pour into the Indian Ocean from the East coast. He was aware, also, that Zanzibar was accessible with a British residence there and many ships sailing the coast between Zanzibar and Aden. "I could not," he said at this time, "answer for it at the day of judgement if I should part with this quarter of Africa before at least some real attempt had been made for the propagation of our holy faith in this part of the continent."[15]

From Massowa, Krapf wrote to the Committee in London, consulting them on his plans to go south and advance on the Oromo people from the east coast. When he arrived at Aden, he found letters authorising his proposed plans. Also, in light of Krapf's immovable vision for Central Africa and the East Coast, the Committee of the CMS separated Ethiopia from the "Mediterranean Mission" and formed the "East Africa Mission." He learned also at Aden, that the University of Tübingen had conferred on him the degree of Ph.D, *honoris causa* for his foundational linguistic work on the Oromo language, primarily for uncovering and collecting ancient Amharic manuscripts.[16] The CMS operations completely ceased in Ethiopia and the only interest it had in that region at the end of the century was the fact that "there Krapf began his life-long labours for Africa."[17]

---

[15] Krapf, *Intelligencer*, 1:388.

[16] Other work had begun on the Oromo language independently of Krapf. Jochen Eber, *Johann Ludwig Krapf: Ein schwäbischer pionier in Ostafrika* (Basel: ArteMedia, 2006), 79. See also P. J. L. Frankl, "Johann Ludwig Krapf and the Birth of Swahili Studies," *Zeitschrift Der Deutschen Morgenländischen Gesellschaft*142, no. 1 (1992): 12–20. Accessed October 3, 2020. http://www.jstor.org/stable/43379871. Also, Smidt, Wolbert. "A remarkable chapter of German research history: the Protestant mission and the Oromo in the nineteenth century" *Cultural Research in Northeastern Africa: German Histories and Stories* (Frankfurt: Frobenius-Institut: Addis Ababa: Goethe-Institut; Mekelle: Mekelle University, 2015), 60–77.

[17] Eugene Stock, *One Hundred Years: Being the Short History of the Church Missionary Society* (London: Church Missionary Society, 1899), 55.

JOHN LEWIS KRAPF, D.D.,
(FROM A DAGUERREOTYPE BY BEARD.)

Dr. Ludwig Krapf, the missionary linguist.
Photo from Jochen Eber

Chapter 6
The Swahili Coast: A Fresh Start

Krapf's time in Ethiopia was, as Eugene Stock, CMS historian put it, "amid many trials and privations, but without visible result."[1] Although he may have been unable to reach any formal, established work for the CMS in Ethiopia, he had distributed a total of 8,000 copies of the Scriptures. It was also in Ethiopia that Krapf's linguistic abilities were honed and identified. He had become more acquainted with the Oromo people and it was in Ethiopia where his strategic missionary mind was formed. As he waited at Aden, therefore, for passage to the Swahili Coast, he was a seasoned missionary, an acclaimed linguist, and a discerning missionary strategist whose approach had been finally recognized by the Society, and now, by a divine providence, he was equipped to pioneer the east coast of Africa for the gospel of Christ. With all the disappointments he had faced, he proved himself a man of indomitable courage and fortitude, and, most of all, a man of faith. "Faith speaks thus," he said,

> Though every mission should disappear in a single day and leave not a trace behind, I would still cleave to mission work with my prayers, my labors, my gifts, with my body and soul; for there is the command of the Lord Jesus Christ, and where that is there is also His promise and His final victory.[2]

---

[1] Eugene Stock, *One Hundred Years: Being the Short History of the Church Missionary Society* (London: Church Missionary Society, 1899), 55.

[2] Paul E. Kretzmann, *The Life of Ludwig Krapf: The Missionary Explorer of East Africa* (Columbus, Ohio: The Book Concern, n.d.), 63–64.

On November 11, 1843, Krapf and his wife set out again from Aden after making preparation "by prayer and meditation."[3] This time, they were going south with direct passage to Zanzibar. After four days being tossed about on the surf, bailing out with some pots and pans that Mrs. Krapf had brought to begin her housekeeping, they reached the harbour at Aden again and were driven back into open sea. Krapf and his wife retired to their cabin to pray, believing they were perishing. They hailed a boat close by but were refused help, and it was only by promises and entreaties that Krapf finally convinced the captain to rescue them. They were pulled on board the relief vessel and returned safely to Aden. They found another ship on November 23, and in the providence of God, the captain, who was from Mombasa, was familiar with the Swahili Coast. Krapf could now see the hand of God in the circumstances of the shipwreck, for now he was able to learn about the people and visit villages as they skirted the Swahili coastline. The voyage, which should have taken a few days, took two months.

For the first week or more, the ship skirted the Arabian coast because there was either no wind or contrary winds. On December 5, 1843, they reached Al Mukalla and then sailed on to Sayhut on the 13th. From Sayhut, they turned due south towards Cape Guardafui, the most westerly point of the Horn of Africa, first sighting it on the 18th. On the 23rd, they passed Mogadishu and began to see a favourable change in the appearance of the coastline with increasing vegetation as they moved towards the Equator. The following day, Christmas Eve, they visited Baraawe and anchored that evening on the estuary of the Webi Jubba River. The following day, they had reached Koyama Island where Krapf met Oromo people for the first time. Had he not felt obliged to pay respects to the Sultan at Zanzibar and the Consul, he later recalled,

---

[3] Krapf, *Travels*, 92.

"I should have decided to stay at [Koyama] and attempt a mission among the [Oromo] on the mainland."[4]

On the 28th, they landed at Takaungu, having passed by Malindi, Watamu, and Kilifi on the Kenyan coast. Krapf's travelogue shows that he was well read on the history of exploration on the Swahili Coast. At Takaungu, the couple changed ships and rested for five days. They were well received and given the only stone house in the village for their stay. For Krapf it was indeed a profitable voyage, especially the delay at Takaungu where he learned for the first time of the Wakamba, the Mijikenda (whom he called the Wanika), the Chagga and the Usambara. He also met Oromo traders who came at certain times to sell ivory and cattle. At Takaungu, he also heard of the "silver mountain," Kilimanjaro, and of a "great lake" inland somewhere, what we now know as Lake Victoria, which John Hanning Speke would find fourteen years later on July 30, 1858. But the time spent at Takaungu proved to be more formative in his plans for the interior, for there, having met for the first time the Mijikenda people, he discovered that they were "more accessible than the Oromo tribes."[5] At this time, he began to adjust his strategy for Central Africa, and this is the first indication that he saw the Mijikenda as the first step towards the evangelisation of Africa, and not the Oromo.[6]

From Takaungu, the next stop was Mombasa, just a few hours down the coast in an Arab dhow. They arrived there on January 3, 1844 and were well received by the governor who entertained them at Fort Jesus. The following day, they moved on towards Zanzibar and arrived there on January 7.

---

[4] Ludwig Krapf, *A Dictionary of the Suahili Language* (London: Trübner and Co. 1882), vii.

[5] Krapf, *Dictionary*, viii.

[6] Scholars like Louise Pirouet referred to Krapf's idea for the Oromo as "pure fantasy." The change of direction from the Oromo people was not a failure to pursue his goal for Central Africa, but a change of tactic, or the insertion of a preliminary step in order to get to the Oromo people. See M. Louise Pirouet, "The legacy of Johann Ludwig Krapf," *International bulletin of missionary research*, No. 2 (April 1, 1999), 23, 69–74.

The Arab Sultan Sayyid-Said (the Imam of Muscat).
Krapf received a cordial welcome from the Sultan and was given
letters of recommendation. Photo from Jochen Eber's Collection.

The Island of Zanzibar was a very significant location in the mid-19th century as the capital of the Arab Sultan Sayyid-Said (the Imam of Muscat) and as a major Arab trading center. Krapf received a very cordial welcome from the Sultan and from both the English and the American Consuls. The American Consul, particularly, Mr. Richard P. Waters an evangelical Christian, invited the Krapfs to live with him while a house was being built for the missionary couple. He also invited them to remain on the island, preach to the Europeans and teach and write books in local languages for the people. It was an enticing prospect, especially since the island climate was conducive to European health and living. But Krapf was determined to move further inland and reach the Oromo people about whom he had talked for so long and for whom he had worked so hard and suffered so much.

Krapf remained at Zanzibar until the beginning of March, "hearing, seeing and learning much," gathering as much information as he could about the coast and the interior. He began also to learn the Swahili language—without a teacher, grammar, or a dictionary. On Sundays, he preached to English and American residents. From Zanzibar, he took short trips up the coast, wondering where best to establish a mission base. He had pegged Yambe, between Mombasa and Zanzibar, in his mind as a good location. He intended, however, to go as far north as Lamu to become more acquainted with the coast, but he was advised against this because the change of wind would prevent his return before November. Uncertain about where he would locate his first mission station, Krapf felt "as one walking in a mist, who can just see far enough to take a step or two at a time."

The Sultan had also warned him of the great danger that accompanied his plan to explore the mainland which had a reputation of lawlessness, cruelty, and violence. In a rather remarkable move, the Sultan also gave Krapf a letter recommending him to those he might meet on the mainland and asked them to help him.

> In the name of God, the most merciful and compassionate, this letter comes from Said the Sultan. To all our friends, governors, and subjects, greeting. This letter is written for a Doctor Krapf, who is a good man and desires to convert the world to God. Treat him kindly: serve him what you can, and everywhere.[7]

It was an unusual letter for a Muslim leader to give to a Christian missionary, but Krapf greatly appreciated his kindness and made his way to Mombasa Island. On the way, he visited the islands of Pemba and Yambe and arrived in Mombasa on March 13th. He remained at Mombasa until the 18th and settled in his mind that this would be the best place to establish a preliminary mission base by which he could then progress into the interior. He looked back to the shipwreck at Aden and saw the hand of God in those adverse circumstances. "I could not help feeling," he said,

> that it was under the guidance of Providence that I had not been permitted to proceed at once to Zanzibar, but had been carried in the second ship to Takaungu. In Zanzibar I could not have learned, heard, or seen nearly so much; and my movements on the coast would have shaped themselves quite differently; nor would the establishment of the mission station have had Mombasa for its starting point.[8]

Although not as prominent as Zanzibar, Mombasa was an important trading centre, and one of a chain of settlements that linked Africa, Arabia, Persia, and India. It had, therefore, a mixture of Indian, African, and Arab traders. Although Portuguese Roman Catholics had established a colony there in the 1600s and claimed thousands of converts, Islam was the ruling religion. In 1840, the ruler of the Omani Empire, Said bin Sultan, moved his

---

[7] Kretzmann, *Missionary Explorer*, 65–66.
[8] Krapf, *Travels*, 97.

capital from Muscat to Zanzibar and traded on the coast with ivory, slaves and copal, an aromatic sap or resin commonly used for incense. Within a few years there were French, German, American and British Consulates established at Zanzibar, but Mombasa Island remained somewhat remote and the mainland unexplored.

This was the mainland on which Krapf had set his mind. He refused the American Consul's kind offer and prepared to move his wife, now expecting their second child, to Mombasa by the first week of May. Soon, after some frustration with his Swahili studies, he was "able to cry 'Eureka!'"[9] He began also to form relations with the Mijikenda chiefs and certain Arab Sheikhs who were able to help him in his language studies. By June 8, 1844, he began a translation of the book of Genesis, and, he said later, "I considered that day, the most important day of my life."[10]

---

[9] Krapf, *Travels*, 107.
[10] Krapf, *Travels*, 108.

Mombasa Harbor with Fort Jesus. Photo, Jochen Eber

Chapter 7

Triumphant in the Shadow of Death

Krapf's sense of satisfaction and accomplishment in finding a promising base and establishing the Swahili translation was very soon overshadowed by tragedy. They had arrived in Mombasa at the beginning of the rainy season and severe rains had brought much sickness to the area. On July 1, 1844, Krapf was attacked by malarial fever. He had somewhat recovered by the 4th, when his wife, now full term with their child, took sick, more seriously than her husband.

On July 6, his wife gave birth to a healthy little girl, but Mrs. Krapf's fever was increasing and Krapf's had returned. When she knew that she would not recover and that she was facing certain death, she opened up to her husband, revealing a fear that she was not ready for death. Her husband, very ill himself, tried to comfort her with the gospel of God's grace and the completeness of Christ's work. While he was reciting Scriptures to her and at the same time praying for wisdom to comfort his dying wife with the right words, the darkness and confusion began to disappear from her face and was replaced with the light and joy of the certainty of the gospel.[1] "Now I believe that the Lord has pardoned me," she said, "He has looked upon me; I feel His presence as I have never felt it before."[2] She prayed aloud for East Africa, for the Sultan, for the inhabitants of Kenya and the mission work, and for her relatives. She bid a touching farewell to her husband and to the servants, especially the Muslim servants, entreating them not to

---

[1] Eugene Stock, "Memoir of Mrs. Krapf" in *Church Missionary Record, detailing the proceedings of the Church Missionary Society* 16, No. 4 (April 1845), 73.

[2] F. Wilkinson, "Johann Ludwig Krapf, A pioneer of African missions," *The missionary review of the world* 5, No. 11 (November 1892): 822–830.

trust in Mohammed for "he cannot help you in the hour of death," but to trust in Jesus Christ, the Son of God who had, her husband wrote, "given her now indescribable peace."[3]

Krapf, lying close by his wife, was again attacked with the fever, without strength to rise or see if his wife was dead or alive. Rosine died on Saturday, July 13, from puerperal fever, due to an infection of the womb. She had some final requests of her husband: first, that he would not publish her journals, for there was too much of self in them, and he should not praise her when writing to the Committee, but to tell them that the Saviour was gracious to her. Also, she requested that she should be buried on the mainland, as Krapf phrased it, "on the wayside leading into the Mijikenda territory"[4] among whom the couple intended to work.

Barely able to rise from his own sickbed, Krapf crossed the estuary at Mombasa harbour, with the governor, to bury his wife. She occupies the first Christian grave in East Africa. When he returned to the island, his little girl, just a few days old had also died, remaining unnamed in the midst of the feverish confusion. He crossed the estuary again on the 15th to lay his little girl beside her mother. Although her life was short—two months short of her twenty-seventh birthday—and her name relatively unknown, Mrs. Rosine Krapf's desire and willingness, her fortitude and faith in the face of death, stand as a monument to succeeding generations of those who would follow her to East Africa. In a letter dated September 2, 1844, Krapf wrote to Mr. Richard P. Waters, the American Consul, a touching detailed account of his wife's deathbed scene. Sometime later, Mr. Waters, "a zealous friend of the mission" and the only one to have distributed Bibles before Krapf's arrival, erected a stone monument over the grave "so that it might always remind the wandering Swahilis and Mijikenda,

---

[3] J. Louis Krapf, *Travels, researches and missionary labors, during an eighteen year's residence in Eastern Africa* (Boston: Ticknor and Fields, 1860), 108.

[4] Krapf, *Travels*, 109.

that here rested a Christian woman who had left father, mother, and home, to labor for the salvation of Africa."[5]

This was a hard blow to Dr. Krapf. He had lost that "human support" that he so much longed for during his time in Shewa. He wrote to a friend, releasing the pain of his loss, saying, "my heart and body wept for many days."[6] Krapf had suffered many losses, his attempts to reach the interior had been thwarted, and yet, still sick and grieving the loss of both wife and child, he could see by faith, in their graves, "the pledge of future triumphs of the Gospel in Africa." He wrote home to his mission:

> Tell the committee that in East Africa there is the lonely grave of one member of the mission connected with your society. This is an indication that you have begun the conflict in this part of the world; and since the conquests of the Church are won over the graves of many of its members, you may be all the more assured that the time has come when you are called to work for the conversion of Africa. Think not of the victims who in this glorious warfare may suffer or fall; only press forward until East and West Africa are united in Christ.[7]

After a period of convalescence, Krapf was soon back at his desk, with great zeal for the study of the Swahili language, traveling the coast, and seeking out a suitable place for a mission station on the mainland. The level of intensity and diligence in the study of the language is seen in the fact that by October he had compiled

---

[5] Krapf, *Travels*, 100, 105, 109. For Waters' work and legacy on Zanzibar, see, Mohammed Al-Mukadam, *A Survey of Diplomatic and Commercial Relations Between the United States and Oman in Zanzibar, 1828–1856* (Unpublished MA Thesis, Portland State University, 1990).

[6] Stock, "Memoir of Mrs. Krapf," 73.

[7] This quote, or part of it, is repeated often, in books and articles on Krapf. This fuller version I retrieved from F. Wilkinson, "Johann Ludwig Krapf, A pioneer of African missions," *The missionary review of the world* 5, No. 11 (November 1892): 826. Wilkinson's work is based on W. Claus' German biography.

an outline of a Swahili dictionary and grammar. The following year, he was able to send a vocabulary and an outline of the grammar along with a translation of the Gospels of Luke and John, to the CMS secretary, for the benefit of missionaries who were shortly to join the East African Mission. This vocabulary and grammar outline was foundational for a larger work, published in Germany in 1850, and expanded again for a publication in London in 1882.

He continued to make plans to penetrate Africa with the gospel. He had already shifted his focus to the Mijikenda and given up on his hopes that "Ormania is the Germany of Africa."[8] He began to calculate and to strategize on how best to conquer Africa for the gospel and establish a Christian testimony, coast to coast across the continent and to indigenise the church in Africa. It was a formidable plan, ahead of its time in some respects, but it shows the biblical insight and innovation of the missionary.

He had learned by experience that isolated, lonely mission stations were not sustainable and what was needed was to "connect Eastern and Western Africa by a chain of missionary stations."[9] He estimated that from the east coast in Kenya to the west coast was 900 leagues. His strategy, as it began to form, was to establish a chain of nine missionary stations across the continent over a period of five years. Each station would have four missionaries and would be one hundred leagues apart, which would approximate a ten to fifteen-day trek between each station. He calculated that this would be an annual expense of four to five thousand pounds.

His strategy also included the establishment of a colony of freed slaves, based in Malindi or Mombasa (like Sierra Leone on the West Coast), who might be employed as assistants in the conversion of the interior tribes. This, also, he said would hasten the demise of the slave trade. Finally, in Krapf's big-picture strategy

---

[8] Krapf, *Travels*, 101.
[9] Krapf, *Travels*, 109.

was the indigenisation of the church in Africa. He looked forward to a day when the church in Africa had its own "black bishop and black clergy,"[10] and, as Professor Omulokoli points out, he "espoused these views before a single convert was won to Jesus Christ."[11] He believed that Christianity and civilization ever go hand in hand, and he looked forward to a time when:

> brother will not sell brother; and when the color of a man's skin no longer excludes him from the office of an evangelist, the traffic in slaves will have had its knell. A black bishop and black clergy of the Protestant Church may erelong become a necessity in the civilization of Africa.

However his plans would develop in the years to come, Krapf had more immediate work to engage his attention and through which he hoped his plans for the continent would be eventually realized. For a good part of the period between July 1844 and June 1846, when his missionary colleague arrived, Krapf was on safari, in an increasingly widening circle, still learning the geography and ethnology of the east coast and searching for a suitable location for a mission station. On August 19, 1844, he made his first trek to the hills of Rabai Kuu (*Old* or *Great* Rabai), in the Mijikenda country. There were two ways to reach Rabai from Mombasa. One could trek through the bush about twenty-five kilometers or take a boat from the estuary, up what is presently called Tudor Creek, that leads close to Rabai Mpya (New Rabai, hereafter *Rabai*). On that first visit, Krapf wrote, "they lifted me out of the boat, and bore me on their shoulders to the land, with singing, dancing, brandishing of arrows, and every other possible mode of rejoicing."[12] Krapf left the village that night impressed by the Mijikenda,

---

[10] Krapf, *Travels*, 111.
[11] Watson A. O. Omulokoli, "The Introduction and Beginning of Christianity in East Africa," the *African Journal of Evangelical Theology* 5, No. 22.2 (2003): 32.
[12] Krapf, *Travels*, 111.

and although they wore little clothing, he said, "they were both quick and well behaved." Yet, he was not convinced it was a suitable place for a mission station.[13]

Over the course of the next two years, Krapf made many trips to Rabai and with the help of a friend Abdalla-Ben-Pisila, whom he had released from prison with the load of ten dollars, he was able also to expand his search for a suitable location. He set out, on January 1, 1845, to make acquaintance with the Wakamba people. By October, he was busy preparing living quarters for the anticipated arrival of a missionary colleague, Johannes Rebmann (1820–1876). As he supervised the construction of Rebmann's living quarters he suffered a severe attack of malaria brought on, he believed, by over-exposure to the sun and was laid up sick for over a month.

On March 25, 1845 he made another trip to Rabai. As he entered the village, the rains came, and they thought the feet of the mzungu (whiteman) had brought welcome rain. He would not, however, take advantage of their superstition, although his friend Abdallah "strengthened them in that conviction."[14] Right from the beginning, from the first time he arrived in Rabai, Krapf made clear his purpose in visiting the village.

> I was neither a soldier nor a merchant, nor an official employed by the Arabian or English governments, nor a traveler, nor ... physician, exorcist, or enchanter; but was a teacher, a book-man, who wished to show the Mijikenda, the Wakamba, the Oromo, and even the Muslims, the right way to salvation in the world to come.

---

[13] For details on how Rabai was chosen as a location for the mission station, see Eugene Stock, "East Africa Mission" in *Church Missionary Record, detailing the proceedings of the Church Missionary Society* 17, No. 1 (January 1846), 1–9.

[14] Krapf, *Travels*, 122.

Rev. Johannes Rebmann. Photo from Jochen Eber's collection. Rebmann remained in Kenya until 1871.

Chapter 8
A Mission Station at Rabai Mpya

On June 10, 1846, twenty-six-year-old Johannes Rebmann arrived in Mombasa. Mr. Rebmann was from Württemberg, the same region in Germany as Krapf and, like Krapf, he had studied at Basel. Although they shared the same month for their birthdays—January—Rebmann was ten years younger. The journey from London to Mombasa took 140 days (four and a half months) and, by the time he had reached his destination, Rebmann had committed to memory the Swahili vocabulary and grammar from the manuscripts that Krapf had forwarded the previous year.

It seems that Krapf's intention was to take Rebmann to Rabai immediately after he arrived, but Rebmann had taken ill with malaria upon arrival. After a few days, when he had regained sufficient strength, the two made their way to Rabai. Krapf had made numerous treks into the interior, surrounding Mombasa, and had visited many villages in search of a suitable place to base the mission. In his own mind, he had settled on Rabai, but he waited until his colleague had arrived before finalising the site and it seems he wanted Rebmann to be united with him in the choice of a location.

Krapf had been there many times and was well received. As he arrived with Rebmann, he asked the same kindness to be shown to his friend and fellow worker. Twelve chiefs had been summoned for the meeting in which Krapf explained the nature of the mission. He had visited the entire region of the Mijikenda, he told them, and was assured that he would be welcomed in every village. However, he continued, "Rabai Mpya seemed to me the place best suited for our object; and that as here I had met with more kindness than anywhere else, I asked them whether they would consent to our establishing ourselves among them."[1] Immediately, and without any further inquiry, they responded with an eager and unanimous "yes!" After assurances of help and protection, and with a few arrangements for housing, the men returned to Mombasa, encouraged at the good providence of God.

In a letter to the Committee, Rebmann, newly arrived and absorbing every impression, wrote:

> It is wonderful to see how Krapf's labors have not been in vain; for this willingness, though little less than a direct manifestation of God in the wilderness, must also, in some measure, be considered as the fruit of his exertions.[2]

The first mission station in East Africa, at Rabai, overlooking Mombasa Island. Photo from Jochen Eber's Collection.

The villagers promised to repair two derelict huts, and so the missionaries returned to Mombasa to wait. They were willing to provide temporary housing for the two men, for, they said, "The

---

[1] J. Louis Krapf, *Travels, researches and missionary labors, during an eighteen year's residence in Eastern Africa* (Boston: Ticknor and Fields, 1860), 125.

[2] Krapf, *Travels*, 126.

birds have nests, and the wzungu too, must have houses."[3] They arranged that August 25, 1846 would be the day that the men would relocate from Mombasa and settle in the village. In the interim, both Krapf and Rebmann were struck with a malarial fever. Krapf made one visit to Rabai to view the progress on the repair of huts and discovered the labourers were delayed because they were working in the fields. On the day arranged to transfer, Krapf awoke with a fever and Rebmann also had not fully recovered from his bout of malaria. They insisted on going, however, and the trek was termed the *Via Delarosa*. Krapf described his journey,

> tottering along by the side of Rebmann, who was likewise very weak and could scarcely walk. We therefore determined to ride by turns on our single donkey, but after some time I was quite unable to go on foot and obliged to monopolize the beast. ... Scarcely ever was a mission begun in such weakness; but so it was to be, that we might neither boast of our own strength, nor our successors forget that, in working out His purposes, God sanctifies even our human infirmities to the fulfilment of His ends.[4]

The village of Rabai consisted of about twenty to twenty-five huts sitting about 900 feet above sea level. There were few wild beasts in this area but many beautiful birds. The cool air was a natural stimulant, and the men found the climate a little more favourable to their health. They also found that the physical labour of building the first houses was beneficial to their health. The villagers were eager to help but the two men, more conversant with stone structures, were keen to lay a solid foundation, and so they dug the foundation themselves.

---

[3] The prefix "m" is the singular, "wa" is the plural = white men.
[4] Krapf, *Travels*, 126.

In October of 1846, about two months after arriving, the two men had completed the first house, in a coconut grove, with a view overlooking the Mombasa harbour and Fort Jesus. The house was twenty-four feet long by eighteen feet, the walls mudded within and without and covered by a makuti roof, made from the woven leaves of the palm trees. They lived a simple lifestyle, but the completion of the house was an important milestone in Krapf's missionary career—a sign that Christianity had begun in East Africa, and that from this house they could begin to expand the mission station with other necessary buildings—a kitchen, stable, storehouse, oven, and especially a hut for public worship. Krapf, himself sums it up in a letter to a friend;

> Every true friend of Christ's kingdom must rejoice over this mission, for it is the first step in the way to the heart of Africa. We have secured a position whence the unexplored regions of the interior can be reached, and the ancient bulwarks of Satan assailed by the messengers of Christ.[5]

Rebmann and Krapf, although single-minded,[6] were very different in character and temperament. Krapf was a pathfinder, a visionary, with an imagination for great achievements and a man of action. Rebmann, by contrast, was content to settle in one place and do his work. By all accounts, however, the two men formed a complementary working relationship and, indeed, a close bond in the early years of the work. A journal entry, two years after Rebmann's arrival, shows something of the heart of Krapf towards his fellow-worker.

---

[5] Paul E. Kretzmann, *The Life of Ludwig Krapf: The Missionary Explorer of East Africa* (Columbus, Ohio: The Book Concern, n.d.), 93.

[6] R.C. Bridges, "Introduction to the Second Edition," *Travels, Researches and Missionary Labors, During an Eighteen Year's residence in Eastern Africa*, Rprt. 1860 (London: Routledge, 1968), 25.

Johann Ludwig Krapf

Today, my dear brother Rebmann began his journey to Chagga, and I accompanied him a short way, committing him to the protection of Almighty God. The feelings which overpowered me at parting are not easily to be described to friends at home … Rebmann turned his face towards the southwest, while I returned to the lonely hut to bear him in my prayerful heart and wish him God speed![7]

Living and working in Rabai was not easy for the two missionaries, especially in understanding and accommodating, as far as they could, the Mijikenda worldview. The practice of polygamy and the production of "palm wine" (coconut wine) were particularly problematic. The coconut tree was protected above all trees and regarded as life-giving.[8] To destroy a coconut tree, Krapf wrote, was "equivalent to matricide, because that tree gives them life and nourishment, as a mother does her child."[9] The power of rituals and customs, and the control of the elders over the people was strong also, and the missionaries were accused of intolerance.[10] Krapf was grieved at the "drunkenness and sensuality, the dullness and indifference."[11] Krapf's, immediate response was indignation. As time went on however, Krapf became less vocal in his opposition to pagan practices. On March 17, 1848 he recorded in his journal:[12]

It was inwardly made manifest to me today, that for some time past I have attacked too fiercely the heathen customs and superstitions of the Mijikenda, the sight of the

---

[7] Krapf, *Travels*, 125.
[8] Henk Waaijenberg, *Mijikenda agriculture in Coast Province of Kenya: peasants in between tradition, ecology and policy* (Unpublished doctoral thesis, Agricultural University in Wageningen, 1994), 227–228.
[9] Krapf, *Travels*, 162.
[10] Elizabeth C. Orchardson, *A Socio-Historical Perspective of the Art and Material Culture of the Mijikenda of Kenya* (Unpublished Ph.D. dissertation, University of London, 1986), 62.
[11] Krapf, *Travels*, 115.
[12] Krapf, *Travels*, 155–156.

abominations moving me to indignation; and that I ought to preach more the love of the Redeemer for His sheep lost, and gone astray, or taken captive by Satan. I must bring them closer to the cross of Christ; show more compassion, and let my words be full of commiseration and pity; looking forward earnestly and prayerfully for the conversion of this hard people, more from God's blessing upon the work than from my own activity.

"Materialism," Krapf added in another place, "completely blunted their perception of everything connected with spiritual religion."[13] Although Krapf and Rebmann lived a simple life, their possessions, scant as they were, appeared very different from those of the village people. The missionaries had to identify people's real needs apart from their desire to have things they saw in Krapf's hut. His house, he said, seemed like a shop from early morning, with a continual stream of requests, and nobody paying. Krapf tended to be generous with his gifts, as an act of love, humility, patience and self-sacrifice. He hoped that his kindness would cause them to inquire concerning the gospel. The problem was, however, that if he gave everything they asked for, it would encourage greed and increase their materialism. If, on the other hand, he refused, it would lead them to conclude that although the mzungu talked often of love and self-denial, yet they did not practice it.

The bulk of the time, in those foundational days, was given to language study. Krapf continued his translation of the Bible while evangelising in the surrounding villages and educating children from the community—or adults, if they came. But the work at Rabai and weekly operations of the mission, for now, was their first priority. A small school was set up, public worship was conducted, with few numbers, and Rebmann led the singing, composing new

---

[13] Krapf, *Travels*, 121.

hymns in the local dialect and accompanying on his flute. One example shows the simplicity of the worship at that time, focused on Christ as the Savior for sinners:

Jesus Christ, make
My heart new;
Thou art my Saviour,
Thou hast forgiven me my sin.
Jesus Christ, make
My heart new.

Also at Rabai, the missionaries tried to set the example of Sabbath keeping. Although he maintained a good relationship with the British officials at Mombasa or at Zanzibar, Krapf felt that they did not maintain a good example in Sabbath keeping or in the use of alcohol and the missionaries tried to set a different standard at Rabai. At first, the Mijikenda would not come to the little worship hut on Sundays unless the missionaries gave them food. Krapf did not want them to come just because they could get food. But even those who would come needed to be reminded that it was Sunday, the day for public worship. They established a practice on Sunday mornings of visiting house to house to remind the villagers that it was Sunday. Sometimes they fired their gun as a signal or rang a bell for services.

Also, to help the villagers think of Sunday as a special day, they found it helpful to embed certain practices on that day to remind and encourage them that it was Siku Kuu (The Great Day), as they called it, a different day, and a day of rest. On that day also, the missionaries bought nothing, did not allow the servants to work, and even wore "holiday clothes ... to enhance the significance of the day."[14] By degrees, using these methods, the Mijikenda people became aware that a Christian spends the Lord's Day "with prayer

---

[14] Krapf, *Travels*, 130.

and meditation on the word of God in peaceful quiet and simplicity."[15]

There was something satisfying about the work at Rabai. Although sickness was never far away and both Krapf and Rebmann suffered frequent attacks of malarial fever, life was simple, and the work was steady and predictable. Death was always probable and never far from their consciousness, but Krapf prayed earnestly that the Lord would preserve his life until the conversion of one soul. But now that Rebmann was there and the base had been established, he was somewhat more content that if he should die there was now in place a man who could carry it on, and this thought gave him immeasurable comfort.[16]

---

[15] Krapf, *Travels*, 130.
[16] Krapf, *Travels*, 128.

Chapter 9
In Pursuit of Unyamwezi

At the beginning of 1847, about six months after their arrival at Rabai, both men traveled to Mombasa to recuperate their health and to visit the Sultan. Krapf lost both his parents in the fall of 1846 and although he had "suffered much and had been often and dangerously ill,"[1] there were also encouragements. Thus, he began 1847 thankful for the developments of the past twelve months. He had welcomed the arrival of Rebmann and had seen the establishment of the first mission station. He had also finished his Swahili dictionary at the end of 1846. At the beginning of the new year, he was contemplating what his workload would look like now that he was released from the demands of editing the dictionary.

He had six areas of focus. First, to make a copy of the recently completed dictionary. Second, to continue his translation of the New Testament and Dr. Barth's *Bible Stories*. Third, to make a daily excursion to the plantation and preach to the workers. Fourth, to continue the school for the children who were interested in attending. Fifth, to devote himself to the Mijikenda and to those from far and wide who came to talk with him. Sixth, to make occasional journeys into the interior to become acquainted with the geographical and ethnological character and languages, and to preach the gospel where possible and thus pave the way for the mission in the interior. An entry in his journal in December 1849 sums up his work at Rabai:

> my daily wanderings among the Mijikenda in the neighborhood of Rabai, preaching the Gospel, and bidding all to the feast prepared, even the kingdom of Heaven; scattering the

---

[1] J. Louis Krapf, *Travels, researches and missionary labors, during an eighteen year's residence in Eastern Africa* (Boston: Ticknor and Fields, 1860), 132.

seed, not disheartened though so little had fallen upon good ground.[2]

In the midst of the busy schedule that had developed around the station at Rabai, Krapf never lost sight of his strategy for the interior. When he first sailed into Zanzibar with his wife at the beginning of 1844, he had looked over the coast south of Mombasa, in present-day Tanzania, to the Usambara mountains. Krapf viewed those mountains as the "ramparts of East-African heathenism"[3] and he longed to break through that rampart with the gospel.

We need to remember that in this era of pioneering missions, the missionary also became a geographer, an ethnographer, an explorer and, often, a linguist. Krapf proved expert in all these.[4] He listened well, observed, and journaled copiously, sending his journals back to the CMS for publication. His insight into the Bantu languages was seminal and, although lacking the finer details, he was well aware of geographical features in the interior and the migration of people groups in East Africa at this time. He had heard of a great "inland sea," known today as Lake Victoria, of mountains with something that resembles silver on the top; we know these today as Mt. Kilimanjaro and Mt. Kenya. Common sense dictated that the many rivers that continued to flow out on the Swahili Coast, even during dry season indicated a continual inland source of fresh water. It did cross Krapf's mind at some point that the silver-like substance reported on the mountains was indeed snow.

He also knew that there was a vast region inland known then as Unyamwezi (in what is today the north-west of region of Tanzania), that was a trading hub. Trade routes had developed

---

[2] Krapf, *Travels*, 169.

[3] Krapf, *Travels*, 338.

[4] Werner Raupp: *Johann Ludwig Krapf. Missionar, Forschungsreisender und Sprachforscher (1810–1881)* in Gerhard Taddey and Rainer Brüning, ed., *Lebensbilder aus Baden-Württemberg* (Stuttgart, 2007), 22:182–226.

between the coast and the interior at the beginning of the 1800s. The Wakamba, for example, were an inland people, but during the 1820s and 1830s were migrating north towards the Matchakos and Kitui regions and were establishing settlements. In the late 1830s, a particularly severe famine forced them towards the coast where they developed further their trade with the Swahili and the Arabs. They also established Kamba communities in the vicinity of Rabai.

With these migrations and the development of trade routes, information began to filter out towards the coast, which enabled Krapf to build a mental picture of the interior. He believed that this region of Unyamwezi was the intersection of the African continent, and from there the chain of mission stations would reach to the west. Not only did the Unyamwezi people form a trading hub for the interior, but Krapf was also assured that there was plenty of water further inland. As he sailed by the mountains of Usambara often on his way to Zanzibar, Krapf's hunger for the interior only grew greater. On one occasion, on a journey to Usambara, he wrote,

> My spirit often urged me to go behind a large tree at a little distance from the village, where I could see into the valleys, as well as the distant Kwavi wilderness, and look upon the high mountains around me, and weep and pray that the Redeemer's kingdom might soon be established in these heights, and that his songs might be heard in these lofty hills; and in full reliance on the promises of God, I took possession of the pagan land for the militant Church of Christ.[5]

Krapf had also convinced the Committee of his vision for the interior and, in one of their periodicals in England, the editor could inform their readers that "the ultimate object which our

---

[5] Eugene Stock, *The missionary career of Dr. Krapf* (London: Church Missionary Society, 1882), 17.

Missionaries had in view, has been to reach Unyamwezi, that interior country where the roads to East Africa and West Africa diverge."[6]

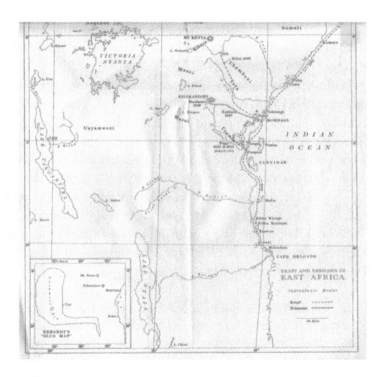

The travels of Krapf and Rebmann in East Africa. Notice the insert of Erhardt's famous "Slug Map," depicting their understanding of what we now know as Lake Victoria. Photo from Jochen Eber's collection.

---

[6] J. L. Krapf, "Missionary Openings in East Africa" *The Church Missionary Intelligencer, A Monthly Journal of Missionary Information*, ed. Eugene Stock (London: Seeleys, Hatchard and J. Nisbet & Co, 1850), 1:106.

By the beginning of 1847, both Krapf and Rev. Rebmann were ready to expand their explorations beyond the Rabai area and to attempt excursions further inland. However, they needed more workers for the small base that they already had at Rabai and Krapf appealed to the Committee in London to send men to strengthen the work. More workers for the "Mombasa Mission," as it was often called, were being prepared. News of the missionaries at Rabai had already been spreading. The missionaries were hearing reports of other tribes who wanted to welcome them. The Wakamba chief, for example, had visited Rabai when he had traveled to the coast and was somewhat friendly towards the objectives of the mission. "In the course of time," Krapf wrote,

> it became ever more evident to us, impressing itself upon us with all the force of a positive command, that it was our duty not to limit our missionary labors to the coast tribes of the Swahili and Mijikenda, but to keep in mind as well the spiritual darkness of the tribes and nations of inner Africa.

In the three years, therefore, between September 1847 and September 1850, Krapf and Rebmann made six significant journeys into three areas hoping to reach Unyamwezi. Krapf made one journey to Usambara towards the south west and one journey north west to Ukambani.[7] Rebmann made four journeys west to Taita and then beyond Taita to the Chagga region, at the base of Kilimanjaro.

On August 25, 1847, five men from the Taita region came to the coast trading and visited the Rabai station to invite the missionaries to visit. The following month, September 1847, Rebmann headed out towards the Taita Hills (a few miles south of present day Voi). On the first day, they travelled eleven miles.

---

[7] For a brief treatment of these explorations see C.G. Richards, *Krapf: Missionary & Explorer* (London: Thomas Nelson and Sons Ltd, 1950).

They made good progress, bivouacking each night along the way. Large stretches of the journey took them through wilderness where, at that time, Masai and Oromo hunters operated. They reached Kajiaro in safety on October 19 and remained a few days before making the return journey. Rebmann reported on his return that the way is clear to form a station at Taita. This was encouraging news and both men made plans for further expeditions in 1848. They agreed that Krapf would journey to the region south of Mombasa, to Usambara, while Rebmann would build on his success at Taita. Rebmann made three more trips, each time going further into the Chagga region—April 1848, November 1848 and April 1849.

On April 27, 1848 Rebmann left again for Chagga. He took gifts with him: knives, scissors, needles and thread for king Masaki of Kilema and was very well received. On this trip, May 11, he saw the snow-caps of Kilimanjaro for the first time and was pleased to discover that the Chagga lived in a healthy environment with ample water supplied by the snows of Kilimanjaro. On November 14, 1848, Rebmann left again for Chagga, with Bwana Kheri, his trusted guide, and a party of fifteen porters. This time, they set out armed with bows to meet Mamkinga whom Rebmann had heard was the greatest of the Chagga kings. When they arrived at Kilema on December 7 and greeted Masaki, the king, Rebmann was well received again until Masaki discovered that he was on his way to meet another king. Masaki did not want to share the gifts with another king. As it happened, some of Mamkinga's soldiers were at Kilema and, after a delay of some days and relinquishing a number of the gifts, he was allowed to proceed on his journey.

They arrived at the boundary of Mamkinga's territory on January 6, 1849 and were very happy with the reception king Mamkinga gave them. It was not the gifts the king was interested in, Rebmann wrote in his journal with some surprise, "it was evident that he cared more about me than about my presents." Both Krapf

and Rebmann were encouraged with the friendship that was beginning to form at Chagga and with each successive king as Rebmann penetrated further into the interior. Both Taita and Chagga
had proved friendly toward Rebmann. Krapf also had found a
welcome at Usambara when he visited in July and August 1848.
With a guide and seven porters, he carried gifts of cloth, beads,
knives, and other articles for Kimweri, king of Usambara. Krapf
and Kimweri quickly formed a friendship and Krapf was welcomed back. Krapf wrote to the Secretary of the CMS, Rev. Henry
Venn, at the beginning of 1849,

> In our journeys into the interior we invariably enjoyed the
> rich blessing and mighty protection of our Heavenly Master
> in such a manner, that we feel our hearts stirred up anew to
> extend our evangelical pioneering to the remotest regions
> of Central Africa.[8]

The remainder of 1849 looked hopeful. Rebmann was so excited about the friendliness of the Chagga that he began to think
about going further into Chagga territory. He left on April 6, 1849
with a party of thirty, carrying presents and hoping to visit his
friend Memkinga along the way. From the beginning, the trip was
fraught with difficulty. Rebmann, too eager to push ahead, had left
at the beginning of rainy season. Heavy rains made travelling difficult, the rivers were swelled, and, with no tents, the party spent
nights under banana leaves. Rebmann's umbrella shielded him
from the sun in daytime and the rain at night.

When Rebmann's party arrived at Mamkinga's, place, it soon
became clear that Mamkinga was not pleased that Rebmann was
planning to travel on to Unyamwezi, and he would not let Rebmann continue. Soon, he was demanding the presents for himself
that Rebmann was carrying for Unyamwezi. In the end, Rebmann

---

[8] Krapf, *Intelligencer*, 1:54.

was left with nothing. He could not suppress his tears at what Mamkinga was doing, for he had been so friendly before. To compound the problem, Rebmann fell ill with malaria and dysentery. Stripped of his health and all his goods, Rebmann was forced to set out for home with nothing, except an old ivory tusk that he had been given to trade for food.

As the party of travellers got closer to Rabai and the food was diminished, Rebmann's health declined to the point they thought he would not survive to see home. He ordered most of his party to go ahead and wrote a note for Krapf to send a "bottle of wine and some biscuits"[9] that would give him strength to finish the journey. A friendly village, however, fed the beleaguered missionary and he found enough strength to continue, gratefully meeting the men returning with fresh supplies.

This journey was a devastating blow to Rebmann. He had made so much progress and had come so close to opening a way to the interior. When he reached his hut at Rabai, seriously ill and weary from the journey, he was encouraged to find that two fellow labourers had joined the "family" at Rabai. He wrote, "I found our family increased by two new members, missionaries Rev. Johannes Erhardt and Johann Wagner. They had arrived a few weeks before from Europe."

The Committee had sent two men out to strengthen the work, Rev. Johann Jakob Erhardt (1823–1901), an ordained minister and a tradesman, Mr. Johannes Wagner. On June 10, 1848 Krapf received a communication from Mombasa that the pair had arrived. He travelled down to the coast the following day to greet them and found Erhardt very ill. He advised him to get to Rabai as soon as possible for the cooler climate, but his condition continued to worsen, much worse than Krapf and Rebmann had suffered back in 1846, and Krapf feared he would die. Wagner then

---

[9] Krapf, *Travels*, 213.

contracted malaria and while Erhardt began to recover, Wagner began to sink deeper and deeper into the fever until finally, on August 1, 1849, Krapf wrote in his journal, "Our dear brother Johannes Wagner ended his sufferings yesterday, and was summoned into a better world by the Lord and Giver of Life."[10]

With the arrival of these brethren, Krapf wrote, "my house has become a complete hospital."[11] In addition, Rebmann's return brought disappointing news after three Chagga expeditions, and was followed closely by the death of a fellow-labourer which no doubt had its effect on Krapf. It seemed "incomprehensible at first," he wrote, and his hopes to push further into the interior were dying. Krapf, however, was undaunted, for he saw the hand of God in the burial of Wagner. "Wagner's very death," he wrote,

> has brought a blessing to the Mijikenda, and although dead, he still speaks to them; for they have now, for the first time, seen the death and burial of a Christian, whose joyful hope is in Christ, the life and the resurrection.[12]

The people who dug the grave and those who gathered around to observe heard Krapf preach from 1 Thessalonians 4:13 and "recognized," he said, "the marked distinction between Christianity and the horrible wailing and other dark practices of heathenism; and so in this way, our departed friend did not come in vain into this benighted land."

Erhardt had studied at Basel, like Krapf and Rebmann, but he had finished his studies at Islington, England, the seminary of the CMS and was later ordained by the Anglican Church. His arrival was a great encouragement to the work at Rabai, especially so since he had some medical knowledge. Sending Erhardt and

[10] Krapf, *Travels*, 168.
[11] Krapf, *Travels*, 168.
[12] Krapf, *Travels*, 168.

Wagner also indicated that the Committee was still committed to Krapf's vision for the interior.[13] The work continued and plans for another excursion were beginning to form. Krapf and Rebmann had been thinking for a long time about Ukambani and the Wakamba people who lived mostly to the north west of Rabai. They were a trading people, travelling over a large part of East Africa and Krapf had long believed that because of their trading and travelling, they would be a good tribe to become acquainted with. The missionaries had already met with a Wakamba chief in July of 1848, and they had been invited to visit Ukambani. Krapf possibly also harboured some thought that Ukambani would lead eventually to Unyamwezi.

On September 18, 1849, then, Krapf began preparing for a journey to Ukambani. He arranged a troop of Mijikenda for the trip, promising them eight dollars each for accompanying him to Kakunda, "the village of Kivoi, the chief of the Wakamba tribe Kitui."[14] He set out on November 1, 1849, and, as they would often do, Rebmann accompanied his fellow-laborer on the first day of the journey. It was his intention to meet with Kivoi at Kitui and then to continue on with him to the Tana River, which then formed part of the boundary of Ukambani. The first few days of the journey were difficult; at places the brush was so thick that they had to creep on their hands and knees. Lack of water and dissension among the porters delayed the party.

On November 14, after a few days without water, they spotted what they deemed to be palm trees against the setting sun and Krapf was convinced it was the Tsavo River. He was growing impatient and encouraged his party to quicken the pace so they could reach the river before nightfall. They were thankful that,

<hr>

[13] R.C. Bridges, "Introduction to the Second Edition," *Travels, Researches and Missionary Labors, During an Eighteen Year's residence in Eastern Africa*, Rprt. 1860 (London: Routledge, 1968), 25.

[14] Krapf, *Travels*, 169.

within a short time, they had reached the cool fresh waters of the river Tsavo. Krapf was surprised and disconcerted by fresh footprints of men and goats and the embers of their fires, undoubtedly traces of a Masai hunting party, which they had just missed. If the porters had not been quarrelling, they would, no doubt, have arrived while the Maasai hunters were still at the river. There, on the banks of the Tsavo River, Krapf learned to thank God once again for his preserving providences even in the delays that so often caused him frustration.

Having finally made it to the Chief of Kitui on November 26, Krapf and his party spent an uneventful time there. Krapf informed him that the object of his journey was to inquire if the Wakamba would welcome Christian instructors "who would teach them the way to true happiness through the knowledge of God and His Son Jesus Christ."[15] He asked for nothing in return but food and drink while they remained there. The chief replied, "I understand your object, and you shall receive all that you desire," and after the Muslims among Krapf's porters had slaughtered a cow, they divided it between Kivoi's family and Krapf's party.

On December 3, Krapf started back towards Rabai and in eighteen days of uneventful trekking, he had, he said, "the pleasure of rejoining once more my dear fellow-laborers, Rebmann and Erhardt, and of telling them what I had seen and heard in the past fifty-one days, and what the Father of all mercies had done for me."[16]

---

[15] Krapf, *Travels*, 239.
[16] Krapf, *Travels*, 143.

Chapter 10
On Furlough in Europe

Krapf returned from Ukambani on December 21, 1849 in good spirits. He had been well received at Kitui and he knew that he would be welcomed back. He had been buoyed by the success of the previous Usambara journey also, but the connection with the Wakamba traders, Krapf thought, offered greater and more promising opportunity to reach Unyamwezi. Rebmann, on the other hand, was less optimistic. He had suffered serious losses at Chagga, from which he would never recover. Rebmann stayed in Rabai for over twenty more years and never made another journey to the interior. The situation at Rabai was not as optimistic either, in the fact Krapf knew that so little of the seed sown "had fallen on good ground." In the four years at Rabai only one soul, a cripple, named Mringe, showed signs of conversion.

Although only forty years old, Krapf had suffered much in the thirteen years he had spent in Africa without a furlough. He had lost his wife and two children, frequent and prolonged attacks of malaria and dysentery, long periods of hunger during hard treks to the interior, shipwrecked off Aden, sun stroke and exhaustion, he had been attacked by wild animals and had spent long chilly nights in wet clothes. All of this had left its mark on his mind and body, and his health was failing.

His decision to return to Europe, therefore, in 1850, would accomplish several necessary ends. First, and perhaps most importantly, to restore his health. Second, to push forward his plans for the interior with the Committee. He had written to the Committee in 1849 complaining that the lack of finances was a hindrance to the progress of the work. He had offered, on behalf of the Society, to get involved in the lucrative ivory trade on which his Wakamba friends were making so much money.[1] Furthermore, the reports of geographical discoveries had roused a great interest in Europe. On one hand, this had garnered great criticism, but it had also brought with it added support to the work of the mission. It would be good for Krapf to visit London, meet the Committee face to face for the first time, and generate greater interest in the push towards Unyamwezi.

Before he returned to Europe, however, Krapf wanted to undertake a survey of the east coast, south of Mombasa. He had sailed to and from Zanzibar many times, but he had never had occasion to examine the coast or to venture further south. On this particular trip, Krapf, along with Erhardt, hired a skipper with a small Swahili vessel that would allow him to hug the coast as far as the Portuguese settlement at Mozambique, stopping in "all the important havens and towns, or villages, south of Mombasa, as far as Cape Delgado."[2]

On February 2, the small party left Mombasa and moved slowly down the coast. Krapf saw again the mountains of the Usambara and praised God that since first seeing them, he had taken the gospel to that region. On February 11, he sailed into the estuary at Pangani and spent the night there. The following day, sailing past the Island of Zanzibar towards Dar es Salam, he began to see a coast that he had not seen before and to meet tribes he had not yet met or heard of.

On February 12, a violent north wind forced them to remain at Dar es Salam where they had anchored the previous evening. For the next few days, the wind was contrary, but by the 21st they had reached Kilwa Kisiwani island. The Portuguese had landed on this island in 1505 and built a fort but did not stay long because of

---

[1] R.C. Bridges, "Introduction to the Second Edition," *Travels, Researches and Missionary Labors, During an Eighteen Year's residence in Eastern Africa*, Rprt. 1860 (London: Routledge, 1968), 26.

[2] J. Louis Krapf, *Travels, researches and missionary labors, during an eighteen year's residence in Eastern Africa* (Boston: Ticknor and Fields, 1860), 335–336.

the unfavorable climate. Like the Swahili Coast, the island of Kilwa Kisiwani also contained evidence of an extensive Islamic population, particularly the ruins of the Egyptian styled Great Mosque. As Krapf wandered through the ruins of the Portuguese fort and the Islamic mosque, his mind returned again to the "colony of slaves" idea. "The best thing that could be done with Kilwa Island," he said,

> would be to establish on it a colony like that of Sierra Leone; as in such a colony, slaves captured at sea by the English might be settled, instructed, and made useful in aiding the civilization of Eastern Africa.[3]

As they continued south the following day, toward Lindi, they found a friendly welcome—the governor who had heard of the work at Rabai invited Krapf to stay and "build a house and do whatever you please."[4] The coast further south in Mozambique was under the rulership of the Portuguese. They finally reached the Cape Delgado and were glad to have completed the voyage, for as the journey proceeded it grew increasingly difficult; "day after day," Krapf said, "we had felt more and more the hardships of our life on board ship as our food was becoming more scanty and poorer, and the increasing rain was a source of continual annoyance."[5] Once they had reached Cape Delgado, Krapf had seen what he wanted to see, and they wasted no time on the return voyage.

Krapf left Erhardt at Zanzibar and started out for Europe on April 10, arriving at Aden on April 26, and, on June 10, he sailed into Trieste, Italy. Once in Europe, Krapf kept himself busy with his publishing work at Tübingen Press. At this time, he published

---

[3] Krapf, *Travels*, 347.
[4] Krapf, *Travels*, 348.
[5] Krapf, *Travels*, 350.

his well-known *Vocabulary of Six African Languages,* his translation of Mark's Gospel in Kikamba, and an outline grammar of
Kiswahili. He was also busy in correspondence with geographers
and geographical societies regarding his reports of snow on Mt.
Kilimanjaro and Mt. Kenya, which was coming under severe, hy-
per-critical scrutiny, especially from William Desborough Cooley, the Irish armchair geographer. Page after page of Cooley's *Inner Africa Laid Open,* published in 1852, breathed sarcasm, disap-
proval and intemperate criticism. Regarding Krapf's reports of
sighting Mt. Kenya with its snow-capped peaks, Cooley said that
they were "wretchedly jejune accounts."[6] In another place he
wrote of Krapf's journal,

> miserably poor in facts, he is profuse of theory, his distances
> are exaggerated, his bearings all in disorder, his etymologies
> puerile, and he seems to want altogether those habits of
> mental accuracy without which active reason is a dangerous
> faculty.

Concerning Rebmann's reports of the snow-capped Kilimanjaro, often shrouded in mystery and the news that Chagga people
had climbed to the snow but most of the team had been lost and
one returned severely frostbitten—Cooley states;

> Statements such as these, betraying weak powers of obser-
> vation, strong fancy, an eager craving for wonders, and
> childish reasoning, could not fail to awaken mistrust by
> their intrinsic demerits, even if there were no testimony op-
> posed to them.[7]

---

[6] William Desborough Cooley, *Inner Africa Laid Open, In an Attempt to Trace the
Chief Lines of Communication Across that Continent South of the Equator,* (London:
Longman, Brown, Green and Longmans, 1852), 109.

[7] Cooley, *Inner Africa,* 92.

While Cooley and others were criticizing, the news coming from the East Africa Mission since 1848–1849 was being published in full-length reports, raising awareness of the work. The report of geographical interest had given Krapf a certain celebrity status, and he received the silver medal from The Société de Géographie in Paris for his contributions to the science of geography. Krapf was in high demand. A few days after arriving at Berlin, Krapf was taken to visit Baron Humboldt. The King of Prussia, Frederick William IV, invited him for dinner, and it was reported that the King and Krapf enjoyed their meal, dominating the conversation on geography and linguistics. Later, the king took Krapf aside to speak on religious matters, and before he left, it was reported that the King awarded Krapf the gold medal of the order *Pour le Mérite.*[8]

The reception in London was similar to that of Berlin. Prince Albert invited Krapf to Windsor and gave him a gift to deliver to the Imam at Zanzibar—a sign, not only of gratitude to the Imam for helping Krapf, but also of respect and trust in the missionary. The CMS enjoyed added recognition in England from Krapf's travels, as Livingstone would later bring to the London Missionary Society. After years of struggling to recruit labourers for the field, the CMS had brought in more recruits in 1850 than any previous year. In 1849, the Society also appreciated a 25 percent increase in the finances from the average figure of the previous decade.[9]

Krapf was a thinker, a missionary strategist and a true trailblazer. Having pioneered the East African Mission and the Anglican missionary cause in East Africa, Krapf, now meeting the Committee face to face for the first time, pressed them, against precedent, to agree to push forward into the interior, rather than

[8] Reginald Coupland, *East Africa and its Invaders. From the earliest Times to the Death of Seyyid Said in 1856* (New York: Russell and Russell Inc., 1965), 401.

[9] Bridges, *Introduction*, 25.

settle at Rabai. He had gone, with the intention, to advocate in person with the Committee for a chain of mission stations across Africa.

The reports that Krapf brought home, says Eugene Stock,

> excited the keenest interest in missionary circles, in England, and the impression was deepened by personal intercourse with the man, whom the committee and their friends now saw face to face for the first time, and whose ardent enthusiasm and single-eyed devotion to the Lord's service kindled all hearts with hope that the time to favour Africa, yea the set time, had come.

For the committee, the push for the African interior also sounded a note of defiance against Cardinal Wiseman and the Papal Aggression which was ongoing in the Anglican Community. Evangelical Anglicans viewed the Roman Catholic move to establish Bishoprics in England as an attempt to convert England to Roman Catholicism again. The Intelligencer Editor seized his opportunity to capitalize on the East African Mission plans. "We shall show her [Rome]," he wrote, "that, although rotten branches may fall off, the English nation, like our own country oak, is sound at heart; that there is life in the English Church, for there is growth in the extremities." The "extremities," of course, was a reference to mission works, and CMS was proud to showcase Krapf's work in East Africa, believing that "the most effective weapon in Church defence is Church extension."

Krapf had enough experience behind him by 1851 and the Committee had vision enough to see the need to reach out, explore and trailblaze. It whole-heartedly agreed, therefore, to support Krapf. They believed that the time had come for the realisation for Krapf's "magnificent conception of an equatorial line of missions stretching right across the continent."[10] But Krapf knew the agreement was not a foregone conclusion and that the committee would weigh each issue carefully. The Committee was cautious not to be caught up in some ostentatious scheme or fanciful idea of an enthusiast, especially at the expense of lives. The Committee agreed however, they had listened to his idea, his work and his perseverance had recommended him to the Committee's approval. Their decision, as one writer put it, "was a tribute to Krapf."[11]

They agreed, first, because the discovery of snow-capped mountains further inland indicated a healthier climate than the coast. Second, there was evidence that the threat of the Masai warriors, who were fierce and menacing, had been reduced. They believed, thirdly, that the powerful non-Islam chiefs would protect the missionaries, as was the case for Krapf's friend in Ukambani. Fourth, Krapf's work on the Bantu languages had identified a close relationship between the languages, and the Committee believed this would make moving among the tribes much easier. Also, the CMS had made significant progress in West Africa at the Yoruba Mission at this time, and perhaps they were encouraged to make the much-anticipated connection between Africa's east and west coasts.

Krapf had also secured the help of six new recruits for the East Africa Mission work—three missionaries and three tradesmen. The Committee had caught Krapf's vision and, in a large-hearted gesture, planned with him the "invasion of Central Africa" with specific instructions for him not to settle down in one place, but to "branch out far and wide."[12] The plan, then, specifically indicated that on his return to Rabai, Krapf would pursue the Kamba

---

[10] Stock, *Missionary Career*, 18.
[11] Coupland, *Invaders*, 402.
[12] Eugene Stock, *The Church Missionary Atlas* (London: Church Missionary Society, 1896), 48.

trade routes to the north west that had proven so favourable. Erhardt, with the new labourers, would lead the charge to the southwest through Usambara, which also had shown promise. The Chagga route was put on hold, and Rebmann was to wait at Rabai, in the meantime, where they had hoped to establish a "Christian colony."

It was a time of great excitement for the Committee, for Krapf and the men who were to go with him. The Valedictory Dismissal service, held at the old Parochial School at Islington on January 2, 1851, was seminal. Bishop Harding of Bombay gave the address to the missionaries and Lord Wriothesley Russell brought greetings and a few words from Prince Albert. Rev. John Hambleton of Islington offered the intercessory prayer. The words, however, of Rev. Henry Venn, the honorary secretary and the most influential man in the CSM, were most remembered. His words that evening were an echo of what Krapf had already convinced the Committee, and they, in turn, have echoed through the annals of missionary records: "If Africa is to be penetrated by European missionaries, it must be from the east coast." "Even Livingstone's more important journeys had scarcely begun," Eugene Stock later wrote,

> And it is a remarkable fact that the most famous and successful traveller since that time have almost all proven the truth of Mr. Venn's dictum, by starting on their journeys from the Zanzibar coast. Livingstone, Burton, Speke, Grant, Ven der Decken, as well as other more recent explorers, all travelled from east to west; and from east to west both Cameron and Stanley made their great marches "across Africa."[13]

Two days after the Valedictory Dismissal, Krapf left England with Conrad Diehlmann and Christian Pfefferle; both men had

---

[13] Stock, *Missionary Career*, 2.

studied at Basel and also at Islington. One of the missionary candidates had been withdrawn before they left England. The three tradesmen joined them en route. At Aden, Rev. Conrad Diehlmann's scruples with popery in the Church of England came to a head and he refused to go further. When the remainder of the party arrived at Mombasa, two of the original group had gone, leaving only one missionary, Pfefferle, and three tradesmen; Hagemann, a carpenter, Kaiser, an agriculturalist, and Metzler, a smith. The mission personnel had been doubled and the future was bright.

Chapter 11
Back at Rabai

Krapf along with his party of one new missionary and three tradesmen, arrived back in Rabai in late April, 1851.

They were filled with great enthusiasm and hope. The news from Rabai was also encouraging. Although Mringe, the cripple, had died, the missionaries were thrilled that he had died in Christ. Despite previous doubts, Krapf wrote that he had "since given gratifying proofs of a renewed heart."[1] Mringe was baptized on November 24, 1850 and took the Christian name John. He was the first convert of the East African Mission. Mringe had borne witness to others in the Rabai community and had borne some fruit. His place was filled by Abbe Gunja (whose Christian name was Abraham) and his son Nyondo (who took the name Isaac), and later Abbe Gunja's wife.

Rebmann and Erhardt had also purchased some land at Kisuludini, close to the mission station and had already begun building houses for the newly arrived missionaries. However, fourteen days after their arrival at Rabai, the three tradesmen took sick and Rev. Pfefferle, who was also attacked with a fever, later died. Pfefferle's death was a particularly heavy loss to Krapf; he had endeared himself to the entire mission team with his devotion, humility and prayerful spirit. In Krapf's view, he was "promising so much for the East-African Mission."[2]

This loss of missionary personnel seriously crippled the mission's plans for Ukambani and for Usambara. Krapf had left England with so many hopes resting on these men. To add to his

---

[1] J. Louis Krapf, *Travels, researches and missionary labors, during an eighteen year's residence in Eastern Africa* (Boston: Ticknor and Fields, 1860), 172.

[2] Krapf, *Travels*, 171.

burden, he discovered, on his return, that his fellow-labourers had changed their opinion and were, in principle, opposed to all that the Committee had planned concerning the push for the interior. Krapf sensed that they were avoiding necessary hardships, and, in his mind, building a new house only confirmed this. We can detect a hint of sarcasm in his journal: "so that the two missionaries could now occupy their pretty residence there, while I remained in the old hut."[3]

Disagreement began to deepen between Krapf and his two friends, Rebmann and Erhardt. Letters home to the Committee and to his friend, Dr. Barth, reveal that he was starting to see his plans for the interior were not going to be realised—at least not in his lifetime. "Though I should fall" he wrote,

> It does not matter; for the Lord is king, and will carry on and complete His cause in his own good time. This idea of a chain of missions will yet be taken up by succeeding generations and carried out; for the idea is always conceived tens of years before the deed comes to pass. This idea I bequeath to every missionary coming to East Africa.[4]

In the meantime, Krapf was not disheartened. His instructions from the Committee were to proceed to Ukambani with Pfefferle and to establish a station there. He buried Pfefferle in June, however, and continued to care for the three sick tradesmen who eventually returned home. With an unusual level of determination, Krapf set out again for Ukambani on July 11, 1851, carrying enough supplies to begin a mission station at Yatta.[5] It would be

---

[3] Krapf, *Travels*, 173.

[4] Eugene Stock, *The missionary career of Dr. Krapf* (London: Church Missionary Society, 1882), 22.

[5] See Krapf, *Travels*, 244–298. The Yatta referred to in Krapf's journals appears to be in the area south of Kitui, known today as the Yatta Plateau presently in the region of the Tsavo East National Park, east of the Galana River, in Kitui County.

the longest of his journeys into the interior, the most disastrous, and his last journey to Ukambani.

Krapf's account of this journey fills over fifty pages in his *Travels, Researches and Missionary Labours* published in 1860. We will not cover every day in this account, but some of the details are important and give us an idea of the hardships that the forty-one-year-old missionary had to endure. He left Rabai on July 11 with a caravan of thirty porters led by Mana Zahu. On the second day of the journey, they were joined by one hundred Wakamba returning from the coast and arrived at the Yatta Plateau on July 26. He had arranged that his two Mijikenda servants would return home after a two-month period and, depending on the circumstances, he would either go with them or he would remain at Yatta and establish the station. But the details of his arrival at Yatta were poorly planned. Most of the Mijikenda helpers returned home before they had even finished constructing his living quarters. His shelter, furthermore, was inadequate even for sleeping, let alone eating and reading. He knew that he could not remain in this for another two months, yet neither could he abandon his post at Yatta. His solution, therefore, for the two-month waiting period, was to go further into the interior, and try to reach the Tana River with his old friend Kivoi. After a few days at Yatta, he left one of his trusted servants with the supplies and set out north on the climb towards Kitui.

When he arrived at Kivoi's village, sick and weary from the ascent, he had a couple of weeks to rest while Kivoi settled a dispute with a neighboring tribe. On August 23, Kivoi was ready, with his wives and a large party, to set off for the Tana River. On August 27, they were making good progress with a party of approximately fifty and were close to the Tana River.

Within an hour of the river, however, the party was attacked by a band of robbers emerging from the forest—about 120 strong. As the hostilities developed, Krapf fired his gun twice and only into the air, for he could not bring himself to kill another human being. In the chaos, Kivoi was fatally shot along with a number of his people. Krapf, however, made it to the bushes where he was not discovered. As he emerged from the bushes, he could see with the help of his telescope that the robbers were successful and were indeed carrying off his supplies. As evening approached, and he was without food and water, Krapf decided to press on in a northerly direction, for he could see the tops of the green trees that lined the river. He made it safely to the river where he could drink, rest, and align his thoughts on how to get back to Rabai.

After darkness had settled in, Krapf had decided that the safest way back to Rabai would be to travel at night. He filled his telescope case, and anything else that would hold water and left his hiding spot at midnight. That night was the first of many long nights of winding his way through scrub and thorns in the dark, aware that at any time he could become a meal for a pride of lions. Indeed, he was so close at one time, that he heard the roar of a lion and the cry of its prey. Starved and thirsty, forced at times to eat wild leaves, he even tried elephant dung, and at last resorted to eating his own gun powder, he travelled on until he saw a couple in the bush. He recognized that they had been with Kivoi's party and approached them. They were at first friendly and took him back to their village, but upon hearing that they were intending to kill him as retribution for the death of their chief, he carried what food he could and escaped again at night.

Finally, after seventeen days of wandering in the wilderness of Ukambani, he came to a friendly village. His clothes were reduced to rags, he was visibly fatigued, thin, and wounded. He was escorted back to Yatta and was reunited with his Mijikenda servant. From Yatta he had another two weeks' trek to reach Rabai, where he arrived on September 30. Rebmann and the others at Rabai were both surprised and gladdened at his arrival for news that he had been killed had already reached the mission station.

After taking some time for recovery, Krapf threw himself back into the work at Rabai. Rebmann got married and, with Erhardt, continued work on the new missionary house at Kisuludini. The Ukambani journey was obviously a harrowing experience, but Krapf was not deterred. He was forced to adjust his plan a little, as he had often done before, but he could still see, some day in the future, a missionary tree planted in Ukambani. At any rate, Krapf was not for settling. He remained in his old hut at Rabai and continued his plans for the interior.

Chagga was closed, and Ukambani now closed also. Usambara remained the only promising route to the interior. On February 10, 1852, Krapf left Rabai again for Fuga, the capital of Usambara, to see if king Kimweri would make good on his promise of land at Tongwe for a mission station. On this trip, Krapf took with him Abbe Gunja, a new convert from Rabai, whom Krapf affectionately referred to as "My Mknika" (a person from the Mijikenda tribe). Others could not understand as Krapf and Abbe Gunja prayed and studied the Scriptures together in their hut at night or heared him pray aloud in their presence. The Muslims who travelled with Krapf's party were especially angry that a Mkifri (an unbeliever) could embrace the gospel, but for Krapf this was a huge encouragement, a great help, and he was especially thrilled for a local travelling partner who "takes delight in the Word of God."[6] For the first time, he had a local believer with whom he could travel and there was a sense of "leisure" in being able to read and discuss the Scriptures with this brother. It was, Krapf wrote in his journal, "a priceless blessing to have even a single person who can understand the missionary, and pursue the same object as he does."[7]

Kimweri, the king of Usambara renewed the offer of a place for Krapf, but his Arab advisors were unhappy. Political

---

[6] Krapf, *Travels*, 306.
[7]

interference and the Muslim leader at Zanzibar leaning on Kimweri called a halt on the European settling in Usambara. In addition to this, Krapf unwisely got caught up in the ongoing political intrigue between the Muslim leaders at Zanzibar and the King of Usambara. Whether unwittingly used by the French Consul, or—as is generally conceded—in an attempt to loosen the Muslim trade stranglehold on Zanzibar, Krapf got drawn into trade deals between the French and the tribal traders. Krapf, it seems, was naïve about the political maneuvering at Zanzibar and underestimated the power of the Arab domination. He incurred the wrath of both the Sultan and the British consul who gave Krapf a stern rebuke for his "meddling." Little harm was done in the relationship between the Sultan and British relations at Zanzibar, but the whole affair very much discredited Krapf, damaged his reputation, and put an end to the CMS operation in that area.[8]

Early in 1853, Erhardt, who had accompanied Krapf on the first visit, renewed his interest in Usambara, and returned to Pangani, on the coast, in March 1853. Disturbances in the area prevented him going further inland, and the second attempt proved the end of the East Africa Mission in Usambara because of Arab opposition.[9]

---

[8] R.C. Bridges, "Introduction to the Second Edition," *Travels, Researches and Missionary Labors, During an Eighteen Year's residence in Eastern Africa*, Rprt. 1860 (London: Routledge, 1968), 28f. See also: Charles *New, Life, Wanderings, and Labours in East Africa* (London: Hodder and Stoughton, 1873), 7. When Krapf returned with a group of Methodist missionaries in 1861, he was apprehensive of his reception in Zanzibar. His fears proved to be unfounded at that time.

[9] Bridges, *Introduction*, 39.

Chapter 12
A Trial of Faith

By the end of 1853, it appeared that Krapf's plan for the interior of Africa was dead. The three main routes he had tried were now closed: Chagga, Ukambani, and Usambara. His fellow labourers at Rabai had come to oppose the plan, despite direct instruction from the Committee. All attempts to supply men for the mission ended either in death or in their return to Europe. Mission resources also were few, which meant that expeditions were poorly planned and executed. Krapf's political tangle with the Sultan at Zanzibar no doubt also contributed to the difficulties in Usambara. The only other powerful body that could have helped the CMS at this point was the Royal Geographical Society, but at this stage, it too had voiced serious scepticism about the reports of snow on Mts. Kilimanjaro and Kenya and of a great inland sea. Cooley's arm-chair attacks on the missionaries had discredited them and discounted them as viable missionary-explorers.

Krapf's explorations may have suffered because of finance and resources, but what he lacked in sophistication, he made up with courage and tenacity. Indeed, scholars will concede that Krapf's observations of East Africa and his explorations easily compare with later travelers, most notably with David Livingstone.[1] Krapf could endure the hardships of life in Africa, he could endure personal losses and sickness, but perhaps the greatest blow in his

---

[1] See Roy C. Bridges, "Krapf is a familiar figure to most scholars concern with the history of Africa or missionary expansion. Yet his place in the record of missionary work and African geographical exploration is often undervalued in general accounts which quickly and sometimes patronisingly, dismiss him to make way for apparently greater missionaries and explorers like Livingstone, Burton and Stanley," R.C. Bridges, "Introduction to the Second Edition," *Travels, Researches and Missionary Labors, During an Eighteen Year's residence in Eastern Africa*, Rprt. 1860 (London: Routledge, 1968), 7.

entire missionary career was the change of opinion from his fellow labourers.

When Krapf left Rabai in 1850 to return to Europe, both Erhardt and Rebmann were in favour of moving out beyond their own mission station and of making a way to Unyamwezi. Rebmann, of course, had suffered a serious setback at Chagga, but he allowed his misfortune to impede the entire operation. When Krapf returned to Rabai full of enthusiasm and the full backing of the CMS Committee to push ahead to Unyamwezi, Rebmann and Erhardt had changed their minds on the agreed missionary operation and opposed the instructions of the Committee. In a letter dated June 1851, merely two months after he had arrived back at Rabai, Krapf wrote to Dr. Barth. He explained the dissolution of the missionary team and told him that the three tradesmen were lying with a fever between life and death. Despite the lack of missionary personnel, Krapf wrote,

> I stand by my assertion that Africa must be conquered by missionaries; there must be a chain of mission stations between the east and west, though thousands of the combatants fall upon the left hand and ten thousand on the right … From the sanctuary of God a voice says to me, "Fear not life comes through death, resurrection through decay, the establishment of Christ's kingdom through the discomfiture of human undertakings." [2]

His instructions from the Committee were clear,

> not to follow the ordinary methods of conducting a Mission, not to settle down at one place, establish schools, and collect a nucleus of adherents round them, but "to branch

---

[2] Paul E. Kretzmann, *The Life of Ludwig Krapf: The Missionary Explorer of East Africa* (Columbus, Ohio: The Book Concern, n.d.), 98.

out far and wide," witnessing to the Truth in successive tribes and countries.[3]

But Erhardt had gone cold on Usambara, and Rebmann had settled in his mind that expansion was not the way forward but, rather, to build up the Rabai station first. He argued that there were not enough workers for additional stations, not enough "iron" to make a chain strong enough for the "immense weight" of East African heathenism. He wrote to the Committee on March 22, 1851 advising them not to send any more helpers for the time being. In the end, writes East African historian, R. C. Bridges, Krapf's strategy did not fail because he or Rebmann were incompetent explorers or because of the political complications that arose with the authorities at Zanzibar. Krapf's greatest obstacle, writes Bridges, "was the attitude of his own companions."[4]

Krapf remained at Rabai for another eighteen months, engaged in daily ministry of the mission and attempting still to reach out beyond their own station, and hoping for more reinforcements from Europe—but they did not come. Although the dispute was acute and the wound ran deep, Krapf had come to realise that not everyone has the same strength or endurance or is made for the same task. "I clearly see," he said, after the second Ukambani trip, "that not every missionary could undergo such fatigue."[5] He had suffered acutely from his many difficult journeys, developing a bowel condition, which was getting worse as 1853 progressed

---

[3] Eugene Stock, *The missionary career of Dr. Krapf* (London: Church Missionary Society, 1882), 20.

[4] Much of the written history of the mission station at Rabai has favoured Dr. Krapf. He was the pioneer, and the most prominent member of the team. However, Steven Paas' biography of Rebmann adds important balance to the relationship between the two missionaries. Rebmann's contribution to the Rabai mission should not be underestimated. On the differences between Krapf and Rebmann, see Steven Paas, *Johannes Rebmann: A servant of God in Africa before the rise of Western colonialism* (Oregon: Wipf & Stock, 2018), 68–71, 192–197, 253–256.

[5] Stock, *Missionary Career*, 23.

and forced his return to Europe. He left Rabai at the beginning of October and arrived in Europe during Christmas 1853.

In the new year of 1854, Krapf visited the Committee in London to discuss plans for the future of the mission. Everything—all of his plans for Central Africa, his explorations and his many years of suffering—was on the line. The Committee struggled through a careful review of all that had happened in the mission. In the end, they came to the conclusion that they should continue with their plan, and all that had happened was "a trial of their faith rather than an indication of God's will that the enterprise should be abandoned."[6]

Krapf was indeed planning to return to East Africa, but not, it seemed, to Rabai. Although the dispute between Krapf and his colleagues had been resolved early in 1853, Krapf was planning to establish a mission at Taita Hills where Rebmann had been so well received in 1847. Despite the coldness of Rebmann and Erhardt towards the chain of mission stations, and the letters from Rebmann, asking the Committee not to send any more missionaries out, the Committee had not lost confidence in Krapf's idea and was developing a plan to appoint another missionary, Rev. J.G. Deimler, to return with Krapf. Deimler accompanied Krapf back to Rabai where the two could plant a station at Taita and also Usambara. Krapf had already been offered land to plant such a station. This move by the Committee showed again the confidence it had in Krapf as a missionary-explorer. Rebmann and Erhardt could remain at Rabai and settle there, and Krapf could branch out at Taita and Usambara.

The Committee arranged to delay the plan to allow Deimler to travel via Bombay to learn Arabic. Krapf, who had taken on the mantle of a missionary statesman, was delayed in Ethiopia to help his old friend, Samuel Gobat. Gobat had left Ethiopia back in 1837

---

[6] Stock, *Missionary Career*, 24.

and had subsequently become Bishop of Jerusalem, but he had not forgotten the land of his first work. Nor had Krapf. The rejection in Ethiopia back in 1842 had been ecclesiastical, but Bishop Gobat had devised a plan of sending tradesmen, rather than missionaries, to establish an "Industrial Mission." In addition to simply circulating the Scriptures, these men followed their secular calling, but "by their Christian walk and conversation they would let their light shine around them."[7]

Krapf arrived at Massawa on the coast, in June of 1855 and travelled through to Adowa, Gondar, and north-west to Khartoum in Sudan and then down the Nile valley. The conditions in Ethiopia, however, proved more difficult than he had expected. The long trek down the Nile valley and especially crossing the Nubian desert completely shattered his health. He reached Cairo in September in poor health, utterly debilitated. He was forced to come to terms with the realisation that his time in Africa had come to an end.

> On my arrival at Cairo it became clear to me that I could not go on to Rabbai in this suffering condition, nor indeed any longer endure the climate of Africa or present way of life, and that therefore my work in Africa was at an end.[8]

Krapf's own words reveal some of the pathos of the decision he had to make and yet the satisfaction he had in spite of so little tangible fruit.

> So, with deep sorrow, in August, 1855, I bade farewell to the land where I had suffered so much, journeyed so much and experienced so many proofs of the protecting and sustaining hand of God; where, too, I had been permitted to administer to many souls the Word of Life, and to name the Name of

---

[7] Stock, *Missionary Career*, 24.
[8] Krapf, *Travels*, 174–175.

Jesus Christ in places where it had never before been uttered and known. God grant, that the seed so broadcast may not have fallen only on stony places, but may spring up in due season, and bear fruit an hundredfold!

Krapf's return to Europe at the end of 1855 was a big blow to the CMS, not only their operation in East Africa, but also the loss of one of their most gifted and noted missionaries. The CMS was eager to keep Krapf, allowing him time to recover his health. He was offered a position on the Island of Mauritius to teach a colony of freed slaves in preparation for missionary work. But Krapf was exhausted after eighteen years of hardships and travels. He returned to Germany, and although he maintained relationship with the CMS, his active service with the mission ended at the end of 1855.

While Krapf's departure was not the end of the mission, Rebmann remained as the only missionary for the following twelve years, continuing his linguistic work. Erhardt returned to Europe in 1855 and later worked in India where he remained until 1891. The work of the Rabai trio was not in vain. During Erhardt's final years in Rabai, he and Rebmann had worked on a map of East Africa. Not only the areas in which the trio had worked—Usambara, Chagga and Ukambani—but also mapping the interior from reports that they and Krapf had been hearing for many years.

The map, which became famous as the first map of Equatorial Africa, included the snow-capped Mt.'s Kilimanjaro and Kenya, which Rebmann and Krapf had seen with their own eyes, and for which reports they had been heavily criticized. Also, all along the coast of present-day Kenya and Tanzania, the missionaries had long heard reports of a "great inland sea,"[9] and so Erhardt and Rebmann's map included a great inland lake on their map, which resembled a slug. The map was first published in Germany in 1855

---

[9] Krapf, *Travels*, 225.

and in the *Missionary Intelligencer* of the CMS in 1856, becoming known as the "Slug Map." The publication of this map was not only a vote of confidence in the missionaries at Rabai, but it was of major geographical importance for scholars and explorers at that time. Immediately, the Royal Geographical Society funded an exploration to the interior and, as Krapf had suggested years earlier, the best place to start for the interior was Zanzibar. The expedition was led by Richard Burton and John Hanning Speke, and on February 14, 1858, Burton and Speke found Lake Tanganyika. Speke later found what we now know as Lake Victoria, which he believed to be the source of the Nile. In 1863, Speke and James Augustus Grant travelled round the west side of Lake Victoria and finally came to Jinja, the source of the Nile. Equatorial East Africa had been opened up.

After almost twenty years, the work at Rabai was revived in 1874, when Rev. W. Salter Price replaced Rebmann. He had left a small nucleus of believers and, in 1887, a large new stone building was constructed on the site of the mission, now part of the Anglican Church of Kenya (ACK). Rebmann returned to Europe in 1875. His wife had died in 1866 and he had spent the remaining years alone in his hut plodding away on his linguistic work. When Mr. Price found him in 1874, he was blind, his working capacity was greatly reduced, but he continued to persevere. He was finally convinced to return home to Germany where he was well received and cared for, and settled in Kornthal, Germany, where his old friend and colleague, Krapf was living. He died the following year on October 4, 1876 and was buried at Kornthal.[10]

While the work at Rabai had been largely inactive as a pioneer work, Rebmann laboured alone for many years in the immediate vicinity of Rabai. Before he left, he had gathered a little band of Mijikenda converts, which formed a Christian church. Abbe

---

[10] Paas, *Rebmann*, 139–166.

Gunga and his son had been baptised in 1860 and the following year, Easter Sunday 1861, another four were baptised. In 1862, Rebmann reported that another six or seven "new enquirers" had enrolled to learn about the Christian faith. It was this nucleus, writes the Kenyan scholar, Watson Omulokoli, "which was to serve as the foundation upon which all subsequent efforts in East Africa would be built."[11]

---

[11] Watson Omulokoli, "The Introduction and Beginning of Christianity in East Africa," *The Africa Journal of Evangelical Theology* (February 22, 2003): 29–43.

Chapter 13
Missionary Statesman and Linguist

At the end of 1855, Krapf conceded the heart of Africa to those who would follow. He never accomplished what he set out to do in 1837—at least not directly—or what he had imagined as a teenager when he first thought of the lost multitudes hidden in the interior of Africa and the "white spots"[1] on the map. The story of Krapf's autobiography ended in 1860, and most biographers follow that pattern. Considerably less, therefore, is known about his later life. There are a couple of reasons for this. First, much of his active missionary service in his later years is really the story of other organisations that he had influenced or that he was advising or assisting in some way. Second, the most interesting, motivating, and readable years were over—the journeys, pioneering struggles and adventures—officially, he was now "retired."

While the following years may have been less remarkable, they certainly were no less productive, as he transitioned into the role of a missionary statesman being called on for advice and assistance from missionary organisations around Europe. His health may have been "shattered," as he said, but his spirit was undaunted and his missionary purpose undiminished as he entered into twenty-five years of international influence and leadership.

At age forty-five, then, Krapf settled down to what he thought would be a more sedentary life, most likely expecting to continue his linguistic work. He decided to settle in Kornthal, about fifty kilometers north of his hometown. Kornthal was a pietist settlement, established in 1812, and the place from which his first wife, Rosine, came. This environment suited him much better than the

---

[1] Jochen Eber, *Johann Ludwig Krapf: Ein schwäbischer pionier in Ostafrika* (Basel: ArteMedia, 2006), 15.

changing culture of Tübingen and resembled more, as one writer put it, "the spiritual atmosphere of his youth."[2] Besides this, the quiet environment of Kornthal, with about 500 inhabitants, was a better studying environment for the missionary linguist.

He settled quickly into life in Kornthal, and, in 1856, married Charlotte Pelargus, the learned and pious daughter of Senator Pelargus of Stuttgart. The circumstances and time of Charlotte's death are unclear, but Krapf would marry a third time to Nanette Schmidt von Cannstadt. Dr. Wilhelm Hoffmann, renowned theologian and university professor, requested him to begin working on an account of his life and, in 1858, he published his two-volume autobiography in German and prepared the abridged English one-volume edition that was published in 1860 in London. This work proved very influential as a missionary motivator in Europe.

At least four missionary organisations were directly influenced or assisted by Krapf in the years that followed. In Germany, for example, among his many other influences, Krapf's work led directly to the establishment of the Hermannsburg Mission. This mission was established as far back as 1849 and followed Krapf's initial concept of getting to the Oromo people. In Sweden also, the Swedish Evangelical Missionary Society was founded as a direct result of Krapf's work and began missionary labours in East Africa. Two other missions in which Dr. Krapf was practically involved were the Pilgrim's Mission and the United Methodist Free Church Mission in East Africa.

The Pilgrim's Mission was connected with the Missionary Institution at Chrishona, near Basel.[3] The plan of the Pilgrim's Mission, developed by Bishop Gobat and Mr. Spittler of Basel, was an

---

[2] Steven Paas, "Spiritual Roots," in *Johannes Rebmann: A servant of God in Africa before the rise of Western colonialism* (Oregon: Wipf & Stock, 2018), 25–39.

[3] William Canton, *A History of the British and Foreign Missionary Society* (London: John Murray, 1910), 3:267–270.

attempt to plant twelve mission stations running north-south from Alexandria to Gondar to open up a way to the Oromo people. This scheme was called "The Apostle's Way," because each station would take the name of an Apostle; Alexandria would be St. Matthew and Gondar would be St. Paul. One lady in England pledged one hundred pounds to each station as they were established, but, in the end, just a few of the stations succeeded and the scheme was abandoned in the 1880s for lack of funds. Again, Krapf was to find the African interior impenetrable at this point in history.

The story of the United Methodist Free Church Mission from England is an interesting connection and came about as a direct result of Krapf's biography, printed in London in 1860.[4] Charles Cheetham, the treasurer of the Missionary Committee of the United Methodist Free Church in England, had read the biography and entered into correspondence with Krapf. Krapf was subsequently invited to Manchester in November 1860 and encouraged the Methodist missionary committee to take up the challenge of East Africa. He recommended at least four men to be selected for the work, and he offered himself for two years to accompany them to Africa, teach them the language and help them to select a location. In August 1861 until later in 1862, Krapf spent time in East Africa, helping the United Methodist Free Church become established at Ribe, about twenty kilometers north of Rabai. In this endeavour also, Krapf had to return to Europe early because of a spinal complaint.

Krapf made one final visit to Africa, not as a missionary, but as a translator for the British Expedition to Ethiopia in 1867–1868, which ended in the famous assault on Magdala in April 1868. In 1866, King Theodore II of Ethiopia had taken a group of German and Swiss missionaries captive, along with the British Consul,

---

[4] Charles *New, Life, Wanderings, and Labours in East Africa* (London: Hodder and Stoughton, 1873), 6.

Captain Charles Duncan Cameron, in a political tangle with Queen Victoria of England. It is strange that Krapf agreed to go on this military expedition, especially given his pietist background and his missionary purpose. However, the longer he was out of Africa, the more he missed it and any opportunity to get back was considered viable. Also, Krapf was personally acquainted with many of the missionaries who were being held captive.

In preparation for the expedition, Lieutenant-General Sir Robert Napier, who was leading the expedition, had studied Krapf and Isenberg's *Journals* from 1843 and had noted Krapf's good relationship with Major Harris at Aden. In September 1867, Napier requested that the British Home Office invite Krapf to join the expedition as a translator and guide, and to assist Napier in drawing up proclamations or other necessary documents. Certain conditions were laid down that he would not engage in any missionary enterprises or religious controversy. This was not a condition that a missionary could agree to, and while he understood the rationale behind this condition, i.e. that he would not engage in anything that would distract or interrupt the expedition, yet he could not agree to "absolute silence and indifference."[5] So, after some back and forth between Krapf and the British military, they came to an agreement: Krapf could answer any religious matters if the subject had been initiated by someone else. Other requirements Krapf stipulated included having enough money to care for his family in his absence, an assistant and an Ethiopian student as a courier. With all conditions being met on both sides, Krapf was sent to accompany Colonel Merewether to Massawa and continued on to the interior to gather intelligence on Theodore's activities.

---

[5] *Accounts and Papers of the House of Commons, Abyssinian Expedition*, 19 November 1867–31 July 1868, vol. 43 (London: Her Majesties Stationary Office, 1868), 193.

The demands of the expedition in Ethiopia, however, proved too strenuous for Krapf, as Henry Morton Stanley noted when he arrived to report on the expedition. Krapf was certified medically unfit and relieved of his duties. Napier, however had been so impressed by Krapf that he recommended he receive the full salary, six hundred pounds, even though he had not completed his full term.

Krapf's travelling days were officially over; for the next decade (1870s) he remained at Kornthal and continued his linguistic and publishing work.

The greatest work of Krapf's "retirement years" was not his missionary journeys or the advice and assistance to other organisations. Indeed, much of this work, like "The Apostle's Way" and other operations, finally came to nothing because of lack of funds. Krapf's greatest work, by far, was his linguistic work. Linguistic scholars still look to Krapf's work today as foundational and important in the development of East African languages. To the Mijikenda and the Wakamba at the beginning of his work at Rabai, Krapf had described himself as a "teacher … a book man"[6] and like the preacher in Ecclesiastes (12:9–10), Krapf gave the people "words … even words of truth."

Krapf was responsible for over two dozen dictionaries and translations. He had left Ethiopia in 1843 and had given up on the Oromo as an avenue to Central Africa, but he never gave up on his desire for the Oromo. He had already started a translation of the Oromo New Testament with his assistant, Barkii, while he was at Ankober. Now, he could continue this work. He sent a request to his friends in Ethiopia to buy a slave from captivity and bring him to Kornthal where they could collaborate on a translation of the Bible. The Story of Ruufoo bears telling in its own right. For our purposes, however, we will simply note Krapf's involvement

---

[6] Krapf, *Travels*, 119.

in the latter years of his life, for in the kind providence of God he was given another unique opportunity to reach the Oromo people.[7]

Ruufoo was young; he spoke both Amharic and Oromo and a little Arabic. In time, he was converted to Christ and continued his studies for missionary work at Basel. At his baptism, he took the Christian name "Christian Paulus Ludwig Rufo." In the end, with Ruuoo's help, the first portion of the Bible was produced in the local script rather than the Roman alphabet. Krapf could finally say that the Lord had used him to bring the gospel to the Oromo, however circuitous the route proved to be in the end.

---

[7] Wolbert Smidt, "Ruufoo," *Dictionary of African Biography*: Oxford University Press, 2012. Accessed, April 20, 2020, https://www.oxfordreference.com/view/10.109 3/acref/9780195382075.001.0001/acref-9780195382075-e-1774.

Dr. Krapf, the missionary statesman.
Photo from Jochen Eber's collection

Chapter 14
Death and Legacy

On November 26, 1881, the day before Advent Sunday, Krapf spent the afternoon with his friend Martin Flad. The greater part of the conversation was on the second coming of the Lord Jesus. At one point in the conversation, Krapf commented:

> I am so penetrated by the feeling of the nearness of the Lord's coming that I cannot describe it. He is indeed near; Oh! we ought to redeem the time and hold ourselves in readiness, so that we may be able to say with a good conscience, Yea, come, Lord Jesus, as it will be glorious when our Saviour appears as a conqueror, and His enemies have become His footstool.[1]

Before he went to bed that evening, he continued correcting some proofs for publication. At 9:00 pm, he conducted family devotions and prepared for bed. His wife had been sick in bed and he left her that evening with the words, "Good night dear mamma; the dear Savior be thy pillow, thy canopy, and thy night-watch." He then said goodnight to his daughter and retired to his room and locked the door as was his habit. The following morning, when he did not appear for breakfast, and his daughter could not get into the room. Friends and neighbours eventually found him, after climbing in through a window, undressed for bed, kneeling by his bedside in prayer—as Livingstone had died. He was buried in Kornthal beside his old friend Rebmann, and reports say that there were many hundreds at his funeral; one report claims as many as three thousand.

---

[1] Paul E. Kretzmann, *The Life of Ludwig Krapf: The Missionary Explorer of East Africa* (Columbus, Ohio: The Book Concern, n.d.), 148.

Krapf had finished his active service with the CMS twenty-five years before his death. However, the publication of his *Missionary Career* by Eugene Stock and the CMS in 1882, is an indication of how much the Society held him in regard. Other small works in English appeared later—one in 1900—and a small account of his journeys in Kenya in 1950. Krapf's name, however, would not be remembered in the English-speaking world. He had been too long separated from the English missionary scene; David Livingstone had published his *Missionary Travels* two years before Krapf's appeared in English. Livingstone's work was also backed by the Royal Geographical Society and dedicated to Sir Roderick Impey Murchison, the president of that Society. Krapf was very much overshadowed, therefore, by Livingstone's early explorations. Furthermore, after the initial excitement of the exploratory years of missions (1850–1870s) had waned, the missionary focus shifted to the work of the indigenous Church.

In Germany, however, the influence of Krapf was more visible and more extensive. It has been suggested that Krapf was "impractical," an "enthusiast," and that "for all the heroism of the early East African missionaries it was Livingstone who inspired the missionary interests in East-Africa in the late 19th Century."[2] Pioneers, however, are often the forgotten steppingstones that provide a footing for someone else's success. This was true of Krapf's work in Rabai, and of his explorations in East Africa. He was a visionary with a bold missionary imagination. He was a pathfinder very much ahead of his time, but he was not afraid to attempt the impossible. Many of his contemporaries did not share his vision nor appreciate his heart for Central Africa, and although his story is often compared with that of Livingstone, as a German, he did not enjoy the same appreciation in the English-

---

[2] James Karanja, *The Missionary Movement in Colonial Kenya: The foundation of Africa Inland Church* (Göttingen, Germany: Cuvillier Verlag, 2009), 8, note 40.

speaking world as Livingstone did. Professor Bridges, of Aberdeen University, argues that Krapf's

> place in the record of missionary work and African geographical exploration is often undervalued in general accounts which quickly and sometimes patronisingly, dismiss him to make way for apparently greater missionaries and explorers like Livingstone, Burton and Stanley.

He had suffered much in attempting to open up East Africa and would never see the fruit of it with his own eyes. He did, however, prepare the way for others to follow, like, Charles New, the Methodist, and Peter Scott of the African Inland Mission among many other early missionaries to East Africa. Among his English counterparts of that era, Krapf arguably ranks among the most prominent. The piety of Henry Martyn, the linguistic ability of William Carey, the pioneering spirit of Livingstone or John G. Paton, or the tenacity of C.T. Studd, Krapf's story could contend with the best of them. His story is, as Robert I. Rotberg said, "one of the three or four most significant missionary accounts of nineteenth century Africa."[3]

In 1878, just three years before he died, Krapf could rejoice that the gospel had finally been introduced to Uganda—the region that he had tried so hard to reach, enduring so many natural difficulties and hardships, nor intimidated by wild beasts or marauding hunters. He wrote to the CMS,

> With hearty thanks to God I have read that your missionaries have reached Uganda, and have been well received. No man has more cause for thankfulness than myself. By the

---

[3] Robert I. Rotberg, "General Editor's Preface," *Travels, Researches and Missionary Labors, During an Eighteen Year's residence in Eastern Africa*, Rprt. 1860 (London: Routledge, 1968), 7.

establishment of a mission in the centre of Africa, my urgent wish for the location of a mission chain between East and West Africa, have at least been filled by halfway ... Since 1844 this chain of stations had been an object of thought and prayer, and now I have been permitted to live to see the development of this plan. True, many reverses may trouble your faith, love and patience, but you have the promise of the Lord on your side ... Though many missionaries may fall in the fight, yet the survivors will pass over the slain in the trenches and take this great African fortress for the Lord.

Krapf was not preoccupied with his own story or personal success but on the Kingdom of God. In a letter dated August 30, 1881, just three months before he died, Krapf wrote a lengthy letter to the Committee of the CMS, giving, "a masterly summary of the languages and dialects spoken on the East Coast from Tigray to Cape Delgado."[4] The final paragraphs of that letter sum up the passion of Ludwig Krapf for linguistic and literary work in Africa, his far-sighted vision for the Kingdom of God, and the persistent and unconquerable spirit that enabled him to fulfil his calling—even to death.

There is still much to do in East Africa, but I trust that in ten or twenty years, in God's providence, an extensive literature will be found for the promotion of Christianity ... Real missionaries and their friends must never be discouraged at whatever appearance things may assume from without. They must act like a wise general does. When he is beaten back on one point, he attacks the enemy from another point, according to the plan he has previously laid out. And in all cases true missionaries and their friends must be mindful of the memorable words which were spoken by the French guard at the Battle of Watterloo: "Le garde ne se

---

[4] Eugene Stock, *The missionary career of Dr. Krapf* (London: Church Missionary Society, 1882), 29.

rend pas, elle meurt"—"the guard dies, but does not surrender."

Krapf Memorial at Mkomani Nyali, overlooking Mombasa Harbour.
Photo from Jochen Eber's collection.

Appendix 1
The Deathbed Scene
of Mrs. Rosine Krapf

The following description of the deathbed scene of Mrs. Rosine Krapf was communicated by Krapf in a Letter to Mr. Richard Waters, Esq., the American Consul at Zanzibar, dated Mombasa, September 2, 1844. It was reproduced in the Church Missionary Record, Vol. 16, No. 4 (April 1845).

It was on the night of the 10th of July that my dear partner made me the melancholy communication of her anticipation of her approaching death, which, by the will of God, would compel her soon to take leave of me for this world. Her mind was greatly excited, and she freely vented her feelings and sentiments into the bosom of her husband, who stood weeping at her side. She said that her whole life, in thought, word, and deed, had been spent in selfishness, and that even since converting grace had laid hold of her, many years ago, she had been so remiss in keeping up a living communion with the Lord, that she could scarcely believe He would receive her into the abodes of holiness and glory. Having permitted her for a while to give free expression to her inward feelings, I found that Satan was, in good earnest, at work to eclipse and confuse her constant view of the Lamb of God; and I endeavoured, with hearty sighings for the direction of God's Spirit, to bring home to her mind the climax of the Gospel doctrine, which is the privilege of God's true children.

The passages in St. John's Gospel, 3:16, and his first Epistle, 2:1, &c., recurred forcibly to my mind; and I was enabled, by the grace of God, to explain them to her with cheerfulness; telling her that she should look to Calvary, where stands the document, written in the Saviour's blood, that He will not condemn a poor miserable sinner writhing like a worm at His feet; that He had long ago procured our salvation by His atonement; so that we need not fear our enemies, the flesh and the devil, nor even reason with them; but leave them alone with Him who has pledged His mercy for all our emergencies of life and death.

While I was thus dwelling on the free, perfect, and all-sufficient grace and merit of Christ, as held out in Scripture to contrite and almost despairing sinners, the aridity, darkness, and confusion of her mind gradually disappeared, and heavenly light shone forth in its full radiancy. With tears of joy she exclaimed, "Now I can believe that the Lord has pardoned me; that He will not enter into judgment with me: now I feel His presence, which is so sweet that I have no expression for it." She shook me by the hand and thanked me cordially for the timely advice given to her. Now she had got around the dangerous rocks of doubt, and the cape of peace and good hope of eternity was clear in her sight.

She then prayed for herself, for her friends at home, for the mission cause, especially for this Mission, and the Imam that God might incline his heart to further the eternal welfare of his subjects. Then she called for the servants and addressed them with decision and force. She told them that she was soon to leave them; but that, from love toward their souls, she was constrained to tell them plainly, that there was no other Saviour but Jesus Christ who could support them in the hour of death, and that their Mahomed could never help them, but would leave them to perish; that therefore they should in time give up their error, and seek for God's mercy in Jesus Christ.

Having finished this address to the servants, she gave some directions to myself, telling me that I should never forbear speaking to the people about Christ, and His being the only and true mediator between God and man. Though my words might be forgotten, yet they might, at the hour of death, recur to the mind, and be then a blessing to the hearer, Christ of His mercy being able to pardon a trembling, contrite, and believing Mahomedan sinner as well and as easily as He had pardoned herself. Furthermore, she said, I should not spend my time in mourning for her having left me; but should strive in good earnest to fulfil my duty as a Christian Minister, and to work while it is daytime: as to herself, she was happy, and going home to the Upper Canaan, where we should soon meet again. Lastly, she begged me to give her friends a true account of her last moments, and not to describe her in a light incompatible with strict truth.

She charged me specially to tell all her friends that they should be true and sincere in their Christian profession, as there was so much untruth in one's mind, which the scrutiny of dying moments would bring to light. As to herself, I should tell her friends that the Saviour had looked mercifully upon her, and that she departed as a poor and miserable sinner. Having conversed with her for several midnight hours, being myself harassed by a feverish disposition, and thinking she required rest, I left her alone; but she would not endeavour to rest, saying that her Saviour might come and find her asleep; besides, she found it so sweet to converse with Him in her present happy frame of mind.

In the afternoon of the 10th the fever resumed its former force with increasing vigour, and her brain got so confused that she once arose to leave the house, saying that she wished to go to some place in the country. From that period she spoke little, and that which she uttered was unconnected. On the 12th she continued in the same state. In the course of the evening of that day I was attacked by fever so severely that I was compelled to place her attendance entirely in the hands of the servants. The morning of the 13th found me still confined to my bed; when she, after a severe bodily struggle, was carried off by her Saviour to the better world, where all is bliss and happiness. I heard her frequently call out the name of her beloved mother, whom I then believed to be still alive; but who had fallen asleep in Jesus in November 1843, as I learned from letters which arrived three days after my dear wife's death. At the same time I received the Funeral Sermon which was preached at her mother's grave, and which now arrived at the moment when it was best suited to console myself.

On the 14th of July the mortal remains of my dear partner were deposited on the main land, at her own express wish, as she desired, by this arrangement, to remind the pagan Wonicas, who frequently pass the road by her tomb, of the object which had brought her and myself to this country. Thus she wished to be preaching to them by the lonely spot which encloses her earthly remains. The beloved child followed her mother in the night of the 14th, and was buried at her side on the 15th, both now waiting for the glorious day of resurrection on this distant shore. Well, both are gone to their real home. Be it so, the Lord gave them to me for a time; He has taken them again: His name be glorified for ever and ever!

My heart and body wept for many days; and even now, although the first ebullitions of weeping and grief have passed away, I cannot look back to those days of trial and affliction without weeping; but I have experienced what St. Paul writes to the Corinthians. For as the sufferings of Christ abound in us, so our consolation also aboundeth by Christ. I would not wish that the Lord had otherwise dealt with me and my departed family, than He has actually dealt with us, for His stroke is a blessing, and His chastisement is glory throughout.

Travels of Krapf and Rebmann in East Africa (1847-52)

Expedition	Date	Note
Rebmann's journey to the Taita Hills	Sept. 26–Oct. 25, 1847	Five men from the Taita region had visited Rabai and asked them to come to their village.
Rebmann's first journey to Chagga	April 27–June 11, 1848	They wanted to meet the Chagga people. Rebmann first saw the snow-caped Kilimanjaro (May 11).
Krapf's First journey to Usambara	July 12–Aug. 1848	Krapf and Erhardt met the king of Usambara who welcomed them and promised them land for a mission.
Rebmann's Second journey to Chagga	Nov. 14, 1848–Feb. 16, 1849	To meet the king, well received.
Rebmann's third journey to Chagga	April 6–June 27, 1849	Very disappointing visit. King Memkinga proved to be

		more interested in the presents.
Krapf's first journey to Ukambani	Nov. 1–Dec. 21, 1849	To meet Kivoi, the Chief of the Kitui tribe. Krapf first saw Kilimanjaro on December 4.
Krapf's Journey to Cape Delgado	Feb.–Mar. 1850	Before returning to Europe on furlough, Krapf travelled down the coast on a fact-finding mission.
Krapf's second journey to Ukambani	July 11–September 27, 1851[1]	After his European furlough, Krapf made a second and last trip to Ukambani, where he first saw Mt. Kenya. An almost fatal journey.
Krapf's second journey to Usambara	Feb. 10–April 14, 1852	Krapf was again offered land in Usambara, but political interference destroyed any chances of establishing a mission there.

[1] C.G. Richards incorrectly dates this trip was in 1850. Krapf, however, was on furlough for most of 1850.

Appendix 3

The Development of Krapf's
Missionary Strategy

Prior to 1840, the missionary approach of the CMS in Ethiopia
was to reform the Orthodox Church in the hope that it would then
carry the gospel throughout the country and to the interior. From
the very beginning, Krapf's goal was to get to the interior, it was
not to reform the Orthodox Church. In this, he differed from the
Mission and took the lead in expanding the CMS in East Africa.
As opposition and natural difficulties presented themselves, Krapf
never wavered in that goal. Early in his missionary career in Ethiopia, Krapf had the idea of a chain of missions across Africa. Until
his last days, Krapf still held on to this idea of a chain of missions
into the heart of Africa. The following outline shows how Krapf's
missionary strategy developed and adjusted as it met with various
oppositions.

A Strategy Conceived:

To get to the heart of Africa, Krapf believed that the Oromo people were the best suited to accomplish this end. He developed a
strategy based on what the Lord had done in the Protestant Reformation through Germany. He often referred to this region as "Ormania" analogous, he thought, to "Germania." "To my mind," he
said "Ormania is the Germany of Africa," and at one time said,
"give us the Oromo, and Central Africa is ours" (see Ch. 4).[1]

---

[1] J. Louis Krapf, *Travels, researches and missionary labors, during an eighteen year's
residence in Eastern Africa* (Boston: Ticknor and Fields, 1860), 101.

A Strategy Developed

After numerous attempts to get into Ethiopia and finding his way blocked in all directions, Krapf thought that the best way to Central Africa was through the Swahili Coast at Zanzibar. At that time, taking its lead from Krapf, the CMS formed the East Africa Mission, and Krapf pursued the Oromo people through Mombasa rather than Ethiopia. Later explorers and missionaries followed his lead in approaching Central Africa through the East Coast (see Ch. 4).

A Strategy Adjusted

On his voyage down the Swahili Coast to Zanzibar, Krapf met other tribes, like the Mijikenda and the Wakamba. When he discovered that these tribes were more friendly and were trading with the interior, he adjusted his strategy and worked under the assumption of getting to the interior through these tribes (see Ch. 5).

A Strategy Strengthened

In 1851, the CMS gave its full support for Krapf's strategy and sent more missionaries. Even when it seemed to fail, the Committee never wavered in its support for this plan.

A Strategy Scheduled

When Krapf returned to Rabai in 1852, after his near-fatal Ukambani journey, he realized that his plan for the interior through the Wakamba might take a few more years and with stations closer together. "It may need another three or four years," he said, "and perhaps a station closer first,"[2] but he could still see, some day in the future, a missionary tree planted in Ukambani (see Ch. 11).

---

[2] Eugene Stock, *The missionary career of Dr. Krapf* (London: Church Missionary Society, 1882), 23.

A Strategy Bequeathed

In 1855, Krapf realized that his health would no longer be able to sustain the pressures of life in Africa. He said, "this idea of a chain of missions will yet be taken up by succeeding generations and carried out; for the idea is always conceived tens of years before the deed comes to pass. This idea I bequeath to every missionary coming to East Africa" (see Ch. 11).[3]

---

[3] Stock, *Missionary Career*, 22.

Appendix 4
The Linguistic Influence of
Ludwig Krapf on East Africa

The Roman Catholic Church arrived on the East Coast of Africa in 1498 in the form of the Portuguese explorer, Vasco da Gama. Between 1593 and 1596 the Portuguese built Fort Jesus on Mombasa Island, but they did not go beyond the coast and left in 1698 when Fort Jesus was captured by Saif bin Sultan.

The Arabs had controlled the East Coast since the 9th century. They had built the Great Mosque at Gedi in the thirteenth century, now one of the Kenya National Museum sites. In the centuries of Arab occupation on the East African coast, a Muslim-Bantu community had developed known as the Swahili. This Swahili community stretched along the coast taking in five African countries, Somalia, Kenya, Tanzania and Mozambique and the Comoro Islands. There are over one hundred Swahili sites along the Kenyan coast. The word "Swahili" is of disputed derivation. In his *Outline of the Elements of Kiswahili* (1850) Krapf gave three possible derivations but settled on the most common and preferred possibility, i.e., that "Swahili" is from the Arabic word for "coast."

When Krapf and his wife arrived on the East Coast in 1844, it was important that they should first stop at Zanzibar to meet Said bin Sultan, the ruler of the Omani Empire. Zanzibar was an important trading port in the early to mid-nineteenth century; the Germans, French, British and Americans all had embassies there. Krapf was introduced to the Sultan when he arrived and found him hospitable. Indeed, the Sultan warned Krapf of the great danger that accompanied his plan to explore the mainland—the reputation of lawlessness, cruelty and violence, and in order to provide him with some protection, the Sultan gave Krapf a letter of introduction:

> In the name of God, the most merciful and compassionate, this letter comes from Said the Sultan. To all our friends, governors, and subjects, greeting. This letter is written for a Doctor Krapf, who is a good man and desires to convert the world to God. Behave well to him and be everywhere serviceable to him (*Travels* [1968], 127).

That letter from the ruler of the Muslim Omani Empire had a remarkable significance. The Omani Empire had held off the Portuguese a number of times and Roman Catholicism had therefore no footing on the East Coast. Who was Ludwig Krapf, but a lonely insignificant missionary who presented no threat and with no national identity—a German working for a British missionary society. Yet Krapf penetrated the East Coast of Africa with a powerful message—the gospel—that would capture the hearts of men and women and spread inexorably through the tribes, throughout the nation and across the continent.

As Krapf settled into life on the Swahili Coast, the first task was to become acquainted with the Swahili language (properly called *Kiswahili*). The Swahili was an oral culture with no writing text, although some texts did exist in Arabic script, the earliest dating back to 1652. Krapf had learned some Arabic in Egypt and in his travels in the Red Sea, and this was a great help to him as he began his studies.

His ability to discern and collect important linguistic material in Ethiopia had previously earned him a doctoral degree from the University of Tübingen in 1842. Now in a different environment, he continued his collection of manuscripts and would send them back to Europe. Since Arabic text did exist, although very few, it was not assumed that Krapf would automatically use Roman letters in his translation. Ordinarily, he would have continued with the Arabic script.

But Krapf had given it some thought. "At the commencement of my Suaheli [Swahili] studies," he says in his *Outline of the Elements of Kiswahili* (1850), "I often thought about using the Arabic letters in my translations and other writings, but at last I resolved on the adoption of Roman characters."[1] He reasoned through the advantages of the Roman script.

- First, the Arabic letters were too inconvenient and cumbersome for the African languages.
- Second, he discovered that South African missionaries had already begun to use Roman letters in other Nilotic languages, to which Kiswahili belongs.
- Third, Krapf believed that with "the introduction of Arabic letters a wide door would be opened to [Muslim] proselytism among the inland tribes."
- Fourth, he could see the rise of European influence in Africa and the "Arabic alphabet would only be an encumbrance on the Europeans."
- Lastly, he thought of how much more convenient it would be for the tribes who would be studying European languages.

Krapf's linguist gifts were phenomenal. He had arrived in early January 1844 and by Saturday 8, June he was ready to begin translating the book of Genesis. "I always considered that day," he wrote, "the most important day of my life."[2] The pages of Krapf's translation of Genesis were soon published—claimed as the first

---

[1] Johann Ludwig Krapf, *Outline of the Elements of the Kisuáheli Language, With Special Reference to the Kiníka Dialect,* (Tübigen: Krapf, 1850), 16–17.

[2] J. Louis Krapf, *Travels, researches and missionary labors, during an eighteen year's residence in Eastern Africa* (Boston: Ticknor and Fields, 1860), 108.

printed Swahili text. He published the first Swahili Grammar in the University of Tübingen in 1850 and his *magnum opus* in 1882—his Swahili Dictionary which continues to be highly regarded, not only as a comprehensive Swahili-English lexicon but also for the cultural data supplied in connection with the Swahili terms.

In light of the Muslim domination of the Swahili Coast, it is ironic that Ludwig Krapf, a gifted linguist pioneered East Africa for the Kingdom of God, and that he chose the Roman script when he began to reduce the language to writing—not to mention the multiple other Bantu languages also on which he worked.

Kiswahili became the trading language of East Africa and soon spread throughout the entire Great Lakes Region of East Africa and to parts of Central and South Africa. Today, although East Africa has a large and aggressive Muslim population, Kiswahili is recognised as the *lingua franca* of the East African Community (EAC) and is spoken by millions across East Africa.

Select Bibliography

Krapf, J. Lewis. *Travels, Researches and Missionary Labors During an Eighteen Years' Residence in Eastern Africa*. Boston: Tick nor and Fields, 1860.

_____, *Journals of the Rev. Messrs Isenberg and Krapf, Missionaries of the Church Missionary Society*. London: Seeley, Burnside and Seeley, 1843.

Kretzmann, Paul E. *John Ludwig Krapf: The Missionary Explorer of Northeastern Africa*. Columbus, Ohio: The Book Concern, n.d.

Omulokoli, Watson A.O. "The Introduction and Beginning of Christianity in East Africa." *Africa Journal of Evangelical Theology*, V, No. 22.2 (2003): 29–43.

Pirouet, M. Louise. "The Legacy of Johann Ludwig Krapf. *International Bulletin of Missionary Research*, 23, No. 2 (April, 1999): 69–74.

Richards, G.G. *Krapf: Missionary and Explorer*. London: Thomas Nelson and Sons, 1950.

Stock, Eugene. *One Hundred Years: Being the Short History of the Church Missionary Society*. London: Church Missionary Society, 1899.

_____, *The Missionary Career of Dr. Krapf*. London: Church Missionary House, 1882.

_____, *The Church Missionary Atlas: An Account of the Various Countries in Which the Church Missionary Society Labours and of Its Missionary Operations*. London: The Church Missionary Society, 1896.

Select Bibliography

Wilkinson, F. "Johann Ludwig Krapf, A Pioneer of African Missions." *The Missionary Review of the World,* V, No. 11 (Nov., 1892): 822–830.

Index

A

Abbe Gunga, 98
Aden, 22, 25, 31, 37, 39, 40, 44,
    75, 77, 83, 102
Adowa, 21, 23, 28, 95
Al Mukalla, 40
Alphabet
    Arabic, 125
    Roman, 26, 104, 125
    Semitic Ethiopic (Ge-ez), 26
American Consul at Zanzibar
    47, 48, 113
Amharic
    Ancient MSS discovered, 37
    Bibles, 35
    Language, 104
    Translation work, 24
Ankober, 23, 24, 26, 29, 103
Apostle's Way, The, 101, 103

B

Baraawe, 40
Basel Missionary Institute (Basel
    Mission), xv, 14, 16, 17
Behmen, Jacob, 14
Berlin, 79
Blumhardt, Carl Heinrich, 20,
    21
Blumhardt, Rev. Christian
    Gottlied, 10, 11, 13

C

Cairo, 17, 22, 29, 95

Cameron, Captain Charles
    Duncan, 102
Cape Delgado, 76, 77, 110, 118
Cape Guardafui, 40
Carey, William, 10, 13, 109
Chagga, 4, 41, 59, 67, 68, 69, 71,
    75, 78, 82, 89, 91, 92, 96
Cheetham, Charles, 101
Church Missionary Society
    (CMS), xi, xvi, 1, 3, 96
    Abandoned efforts in
        Ethiopia, 36
    backed Krapf's vision, 92
    benefited from Krapf's
        labours, 79
    East Africa Mission formed,
        37
    Established, 16
    Mediterranean Mission, 19,
        37
    missionary effort in Ethiopia,
        19
    Partnership with the Basel
        Mission, 16
    Seminary in Islington, 16
Coates, Dandeson, 17
Committee (CMS), 33, 37, 65,
    67, 70, 75, 76, 80, 81, 82, 86,
    91, 92, 93, 94
    Committed to Krapf's vision,
        71, 81
    Confidence in Krapf, 94, 120
    Krapf meets, 79
    Krapf's final letter to, 110
    Letter re. the death of Rosine,
        48
    Not to send more
        missionaries, 94

Index

L

M

N

Index

V

Venn, Henry, 69, 82
Voi, 67

W

Wagner, Johann, 70, 71
    Arrives at Rabai, 70
    Death of, 70, 71
    First Christian burial, 71
Wakamba, 65, 72, 87
    Chief Kivoi, 72
    Chief visited Rabai, 67
    First learned of, 41
    First met, 52
    Krapf's intention for the, 73,
        103, 120
    Traders, 75, 76
Wazungu, 57
Watamu, 1, 41

Waters, Richard P., 113
    A friend of the mission, 48
    An evangelical Christian, 43
    Rosine Krapf's monument,
        48
Webi Jubba River, 40
Wolfenhausen, 15

Y

Yambe Island, 43, 44
Yatta, 86, 87, 88
Yerer, Mt., 25
Yoruba Mission, 81

Z

Zanzibar, 37, 40, 41, 43, 44, 45,
    61, 64, 65, 76, 77, 79, 82, 90,
    91, 93, 97, 113, 120, 123

The Krapf Project

RESOURCES FOR RURAL PASTORS

We provide pastors in rural East Africa with ministry resources. Along with ongoing mentorship and seminars, the goal of the Krapf Project is to get the right books in the right hands. We publish a quarterly expository magazine, and books for rural pastors with study guides and teaching plans built in. These resources are designed to develop a culture of reading among the pastors for the long-term good of the Church.

The Krapf Project is an associate ministry with UFM Worldwide.

In partnership with

www.krapfproject.com